Brand Mechanics

The art and science of building brands[SM]

Michael Llewellyn-Williams, PhD

San Francisco

www.chromiumbookssf.com

Published by
Chromium Books
440 Brannan Street
San Francisco, CA 94107

Interior design by Brad Reynolds
Cover design by Tony Wessling

ISBN-13: 978-0615747323 (Chromium Books)
ISBN-10: 0615747329
Library of Congress Control Number: 2012924375

Printed in the United States of America

Table of Contents

About This Book i

About the Author vii

Acknowledgements x

Introduction xi

Chapter Summary xvii

Chapter 1: What is a Brand, Branding and Messaging? 1

Chapter 2: The FBE™ Methodology (Part 1: Logistics) 19

Chapter 3: The FBE™ Methodology (Part 2: Tasks and Overview) 29

Chapter 4: Mission Statement 47

Chapter 5: Deep Human Needs 53

Chapter 6: Provable Superiority 61

Chapter 7: Character/Personality 69

Chapter 8: Source of Trust/Authority 81

Chapter 9: The Future 85

Chapter 10: Future Brand Essence 89

Chapter 11: Brand Vision 105

Chapter 12: Now What? 113

Chapter 13: Future Brand Essence Alignment 121

Chapter 14: Brand Reinforcement and Tracking 135

Chapter 15: Summary: Quiz Time! 149

Appendix 1: Qualitative Research Tools for Brand Understanding 153

Appendix 2: Synectics and Consensus Building 156

Appendix 3: Workshop Icebreakers/Energizers 165

Appendix 4: Puzzles 172

Appendix 5: Answers to Chapter 15 Quiz 175

Appendix 6: Answers to Puzzles 178

Index 181

About This Book

In this book you will learn the art and science of building brands without the fluffy nonsense and BS.

More specifically, you will learn in detail the breakthrough BrandMechanics® proprietary FBE™ Methodology – and discover a simple step-by-step process for creating a powerful brand strategy.

For the first time in print, the author reveals the secrets behind the remarkable process that has generated hundreds of thousands of dollars in revenue from clients in the U.S., U.K., Europe, Asia and Canada, including Disney, Toyota/Scion, Visa, AOL, Boston Consulting Group, Miller Brewing, City of San Jose, McDonald's, Hewlett-Packard, Accenture, Intel, Tomb Raider/Lara Croft, Mandalay Bay Resort & Casino and Pentax Cameras.

You will also learn the shocking truth about the many high-priced advertising and digital agencies, design studios and consulting firms who charge their clients small fortunes for brand strategy development while regularly outsourcing the work and paying a fraction of what they charge, and often delivering an "immersion" in the brand without actually defining it.

The brand that concerns you in particular might be a new brand, an old brand, a large brand, a small brand or one that doesn't even exist in a category that doesn't even exist yet.

It might be a company, a product, a service or simply an idea for a start-up. Or a group of companies products or services. It might be an NGO or a university, a political coalition or a city. It could be a B2C or B2B brand. It may even be you yourself that you want to create a brand for.

Regardless of the kind of brand you wish to create (or even change), the BrandMechanics® FBE™ process will help you achieve your goals without having to resort to high-priced advertising agencies, design studios or consulting firms.

This book, through the intensive process it describes and the tried-and-tested, penetrating questions it poses, will bring fresh clarity and focus to your thinking, and alignment to your organization.

BRAND MECHANICS is written for a variety of audiences:

- Branding, marketing and communications professionals who privately admit they don't know enough about brand strategy and branding to be able to push back and challenge their vendors.

- Brand strategy students who want to quickly understand the fundamentals of brand strategy and begin building a brand.

- Time-crunched, budget-restricted brand owners and stakeholders who are becoming increasingly suspicious of high-priced and long-winded purveyors of brand wisdom.

- Anyone who has been overloaded with so much fluffy nonsense and BS about the subject in the past few years that they're not sure what to think next.

Such people will include:

- CEOs
- CMOs
- Chief Strategy Officers
- Marketing executives
- Entrepreneurs
- Brand consultants
- Agency, design studio and consulting firm strategic planners and brand strategists
- Agency and design studio creative resources
- MBA and communication arts students and faculty

If just one of the following statements is true for you, then you need this book:

- "I need a practical 'how to' hands-on working guide to creating a brand strategy, not another book on brand philosophy."

- "I want to know the best questions to ask to develop a powerful brand strategy."

- "We know what the brand stands for today, but we really need to figure out what we want it to stand for in the future."

- "I don't have a big budget and unlimited time to figure out our brand strategy."

- "We struggle every time we try to write an engaging elevator pitch."

- "If *The Wall Street Journal* asked us, 'What does your brand stand for?' it would be hard to respond with a short, inspiring answer."

- "I need to crystallize this brand into a powerful, focused, memorable idea."

- "So many cool ideas, but we're not all on the same page."

- "Ask anyone working on this brand what it stands for and you'll get different answers – some of them contradictory."

A NOTE ON DIGITAL AND SOCIAL MEDIA

This all sounds great, you might say, but what about digital media, including social media and SEO/SEM? Haven't they rewritten the rules of brand strategy?

While digital media, in all its different flavors, has most definitely transformed the communications landscape in the last 20 years and has caused the venerable Purchase Funnel (awareness leading to familiarity, consideration and purchase) to be rewritten as the more iterative Consumer Journey, the fundamentals of brand strategy development – being necessarily message- and media-neutral – remain virtually unchanged.

To use the simple analogy of a brand as a person:

The number of ways a newborn can grow and develop, what it wants to wear, who it wants to associate with, what opinions it wants to form or embrace, how it wants to conduct itself, where it wants to live, how it wants to help others – all these opportunities continue to multiply.

But the way that babies are born has not changed a great deal (test tube babies, surrogate pregnancies, etc. notwithstanding).

For me, digital media offers five important opportunities:

- Low cost of entry
- Consumer dialog and engagement (as opposed to traditional one-way message distribution), and instant word-of-mouth sharing.
- More focused consumer targeting
- Better quantitative measurement, including general ROI and the more specific $ROI
- Automation of message serving

And there are also pitfalls to avoid:

- While it's generally a good thing to have consumers talking about your brand and giving feedback, it's not a good thing to yield overall control of the brand narrative and allow consumers to potentially dictate to you what your brand wants to be – for example, I can't imagine luxury brands abandoning their premium positions in response to bloggers demanding deep price cuts.

- While freedom of speech is great and encourages brands to be open, honest and authentic, where do you draw the line between welcoming feedback and censoring malicious gossip?

- And while clients will continue to take some degree of comfort from quantitative measurements, a full and reliable system of online ratings capable of populating accurate, econometrics-driven

$ROI calculation models will continue to challenge the best minds in the business until the rapidly evolving digital media ecosystem truly stabilizes.

- Lastly, I believe it would be folly for digital agencies to develop digital creative briefs focused purely on digital behaviors at the expense of basic human behaviors, needs, motivations and values – consumers are, after all, human beings first and digital consumers second.

So while I continue to be a great fan of digital media in all its different flavors, and believe it is much more than "just another communications channel," the art and science of defining a coherent brand strategy remains fundamentally unchanged, which means a book such as this will be necessary for the foreseeable future.

About the Author

Michael Llewellyn-Williams, PhD is the Founder of BrandMechanics®, a brand consulting firm in San Francisco specializing in brand and communications strategy development, but without the fluffy nonsense and BS.

He has been working as a hands-on brand strategist and agency account planner for many years and been a conference speaker/chair in Europe, the United States and Asia.

Dr. Llewellyn-Williams has worked on such famous brands as:

- Accenture
- AOL
- Bank of America
- BMW
- Boston Consulting Group
- City of San Jose Green Initiatives
- Converse
- Disney
- Hewlett-Packard
- Intel
- Kraft
- Land Rover
- La-Z-Boy
- Mandalay Bay Resort & Casino
- McDonald's
- Miller Genuine Draft
- Mini
- Orville Redenbacher
- Pacific Bell
- Partnership for a Drug-Free America
- Pedigree Pet Foods
- Pentax Cameras
- QANTAS
- Scotch/3M
- Shell
- Suntech Power
- Tomb Raider/Lara Croft
- Toyota/Scion
- Visa

Agency experience includes stints at BMP, WCRS, FCB, The Creative Business, KLP, KMM, Ketchum Advertising, Leo Burnett Asia Pacific, Winkler Advertising, Attik, RPA, Scheyer/SF, T3, The Evolution Bureau, Wessling Group and Chromium Brands.

He was elected a Member of the Institute of Practitioners in Advertising in London after only seven years in the industry and was awarded the prestigious Marketing Award for Innovation by that institute in 1990. That same year he was elected to the highly prestigious Marketing Society in London.

He has appeared on U.K. TV discussing advertising, has twice been a judge for The Effies in New York, has been a guest lecturer at the Miami Ad School in San Francisco and has a string of proprietary methodologies to his name.

Other clients include:

- American AgCredit
- Ammo Marketing
- Andalé
- AXA Rosenberg
- Beech Street Capital
- BravoGifts
- 21st Century Insurance
- CAMICO
- Cephren
- Clear Ink
- Committee of 200
- McKinsey
- E-Assist
- Fineman Associates PR
- First Franklin Financial
- First Street
- ForGolf
- Freestyle Interactive
- HelloBrain
- Image Printing Solutions
- Intershop
- Ivus Inc.
- Jesuit School of Theology at Berkeley
- Ketchum PR
- Krupp Brothers Winery
- Las Vegas Springs Preserve
- Mediaplex
- Moroz Vodka
- Mr Stock
- MyHomeLink
- Openwave
- Palo Alto University
- Red Bricks Media
- Red Sky Interactive
- Santa Clara University
- Sendmail
- Stagecoach Vineyard
- Taylor Woodrow Homes
- TeamToolz
- trueAnthem
- Tsubo
- Urban Pioneer
- Winkler Advertising

For Joey, Abby and Savannah,
and the memory of Lady.

Acknowledgements

Thanks to my wife Joey for her patience.

Thanks also to all the clients I have been fortunate to work with and to Tom Freyer, Executive Creative Director at AdPeople, who read the manuscript and made helpful suggestions.

Special thanks to Tony Wessling at Chromium Books for his help with the cover design and constant support in bringing this book to fruition.

— Michael Llewellyn-Williams, PhD
www.brandmechanics.com
San Francisco
January 2013

Introduction

Why do you need a brand strategy?

A powerful brand strategy enables you to:

- Invent the future and make the changes needed for profitable success
- Express your value proposition to your core audiences efficiently and consistently
- Create monetary equity for your brand so your company or product is worth more than its book value
- Engage your employees and ensure everyone is on the same page

Without internal enthusiastic consensus on your brand strategy:

- You have no reliable guide for the future
- No benchmark to measure the consistency of your brand
- You may be doomed to endless debates about what your brand stands for and what you want it to stand for in the future

To quote the late great brand guru Stephen King:

"A product is something that is made in a factory; a brand is something that is bought by a customer.

"A product can be copied by a competitor; a brand is unique.

"A product can be quickly outdated; a successful brand is timeless."

But none of this is really possible without a clearly defined, focused, inspiring brand strategy.

After all, everyone already knows how important it is to have a strong brand. And everyone already knows how important branding is. So what's new?

Actually, there are some dirty little secrets that need to be exposed.

> There are some dirty little secrets that need to be exposed.

Dirty little secret #1:

Many design studios, ad agencies and consulting firms take advantage of their clients.

They claim they can define their client's brand and execute it in branding. What the client actually gets, however, often falls short of what was promised.

Take design studios as an example: Some will deliver to their clients nothing more than a brand identity – a logo, logotype, fonts, color palette and some really spiffy collateral material and design templates – without taking the trouble to define in a concise, highly focused way what the brand wants to stand for in the eyes of its core audiences, and worse, not making it clear that branding is more than just external creative expressions.

Ad agencies, on the other hand, love ads, and many of them are good at making ads – it's what they do best. They don't however always know how to define brands but will say they do in order to make the ads they love so much. So instead of getting a clearly defined brand, the client gets an advertising execution which the agency creative director swears "does a great job for the brand" while the strategy director turns a blind eye.

Consulting firms can sometimes be the worst. They know how to audit and profile a brand at a point in time, and they'll produce a heavy, indigestible report six months later. It's called the "thud factor" or "passing the weight test," and it's designed to impress the client, imbue the findings with unchallengeable authority and justify the ludicrously high fees.

Shamefully missing from all the above is a simple statement of what the brand wants to stand for – the brand's desired essence. I'm not talking about core values, drivers, positioning, strategy or proposition, although all of these are important. I'm talking about the brand's future essence – the brand's desired DNA,

> **Shamefully missing ... is a simple statement of what the brand wants to stand for.**

its spirit, its heart and soul – that's meant to guide every business, marketing and communications strategy and decision-making relating to that brand.

Many of them forget that branding is more than an ad, a design or image metrics. Branding is also a fundamental principle that can bring cohesion to the diversity of an organization's activities and its people.

But despite not knowing how to define a client's brand, many design studios, ad agencies and consulting firms continue to claim they do and get away with it.

Dirty little secret #2:

Flawed deliverables.

The few design studios, ad agencies and consulting firms that do understand brand strategy (and thankfully there are some that do) unfortunately often deliver flawed results. Either too rational, or uninspiring, or generic/undifferentiated, or too long/unmemorable (laundry lists are such a cop-out) – or worse, something that sums up where the brand is *today* rather than where it wants to be in the future.

Their cardinal sin is in failing to tell their clients that they need a *future* brand essence – something that's going to last five to 10 years, something for the organization to

> **In most cases a Brand's Essence is more than just its Persona.**

reach for and align with. Part of their "scam" is that they want to repeat the project every couple of years to earn more money.

Other kinds of flawed deliverables include:

- Brand workshops that are fine for getting participants immersed in the brand but which fail to reach a solid, focused, written conclusion that defines what the brand wants to stand for.

- Presenting with great drama the brand's Persona (a.k.a. its personality/character), accompanied by lots of cute photographs, as the brand's Essence or Soul. Sure, there are some categories (fragrances, fashion, tobacco, etc.) where a brand's Persona is also its Essence, but in most cases a brand's Essence is more than just its Persona.

Dirty little secret #3:

Hiding behind too much jargon.

Firstly, what do all these words have in common?

- Advertising
- Dashboard
- Champion
- Value
- Function
- Mission
- Character
- Identity
- Essence
- Map
- Management
- Positioning
- Vision
- Strategy
- Activation
- Architecture
- Authority
- Strength
- Vision
- Icon
- Weakness
- Consistency
- Platform
- Furniture
- Attribute
- Profile
- Preference
- Loyalty

- Equity
- Benefit
- Audit
- Leader

- Role
- Asset
- Tracking
- Messaging

And secondly, what do all the words on this list have in common?

- Challenger
- Tribal
- Heritage
- Value
- Niche
- Cult
- Specialty
- B2B
- Endorsement
- Monolithic
- Regional

- B2C
- Spoiler
- Me-too
- Luxury
- Master
- Corporate
- Global
- Retail
- Sub
- Mass market
- Ephemeral

With the first list, you can put the word "Brand" in front of any of the words and you'll have one of the multitudes of terms used and abused in the world of brands and branding.

With the second list, you can put the word "Brand" *after* any of the words with a similar result.

These are incomplete lists, but it demonstrates that there are a lot of "brand" terms out there, some of them meaningful and some of them not.

> You don't need to know or understand all these terms in order to develop a powerful brand strategy.

The thing is, you don't need to know or understand all these terms in order to develop a powerful brand strategy. For some of the terms there is not even industry-wide agreement on their definition.

But people in this business love to create jargon because it creates a sense of mystique to make them look smarter than they really are.

Understand that the business of brands and branding is not regulated in the way the legal and medical professions are. You don't have to be certified or licensed to open a studio, agency or branding firm.

Although I'll be referring to several of the BrandMechanics® programs in this book, I've tried to avoid, as far as possible, too much "brand jargon."

Dirty little secret #4:

Brand consultants can be such a mixed bag. I've met a lot of them in my time, and while some of them are very bright many are, in my view, complete charlatans.

With their PhDs in "hindsight," they'll pontificate on what certain (successful) brands did right and how other (ailing) brands screwed up and even draw up immutable laws governing brands. But they're long on post-facto analysis and short on detailed processes for success.

Either they have or they don't have processes. If they do, then they won't want to share it – it's their livelihood and besides, they probably stole it. And if they don't have a process, then their dabbling in brand consulting is an even bigger scam.

That's why this book is needed to reveal what's going on and demonstrate there is an easier way. Read on and you will not only save time and money, but you'll also get better service from your brand partners because you'll be able to ask all the kinds of questions they'd rather you didn't ask.

Chapter Summary

1. **What is a brand, branding and messaging?**

   Some common definitions. The power and financial value of brands. How does messaging differ from brands and branding? Emotional engagement and rational persuasion. Two dangerous words to watch: strategy and positioning. Why Brand Essence is at the top of the brand totem pole.

2. **The FBE™ Methodology — Part 1: Logistics**

   Importance of advance logistical preparation. Calendaring issues and how to address them. Who should participate and why. Choosing the venue. Recommended equipment. What participants can expect.

3. **The FBE™ Methodology — Part 2: Tasks and Overview**

   Review of Brand Audits in general. The roles and importance of the internal and external Brand Audits. The importance of candor in the internal audit. Key questions to be asked. Differences in approach for B2C and B2B external audits. An overview of the FBE™ methodology and the Brand Mirror™.

4. **Mission Statement**

   Its purpose and how companies can get it wrong. What does the brand actually do for its core target audience? The roles of the brand, rational and emotional. The importance of choosing the right "doing words." Testing your Mission Statement.

5. **Deep Human Needs**

   What is a Deep Human Need, and which ones in the core target audience can the brand fulfill? Using the Deep Human Needs approach as a surrogate for target audience needs when consumer research is not a viable option. A list of all the deep human needs you'll probably ever need.

6. Provable Superiority

What makes this brand's performance provably superior to its competitors? Rational benefits. The WCRS mantra for product interrogation. Why it's not always a good idea to accept the client's view that their product or service has no superiority.

7. Character/Personality

Why should the core target audience like this brand? Why character/personality is an important benchmark for brand consistency and fundamental in categories like apparel, alcohol, fragrances and tobacco. A list of useful words and phrases. Words that are best avoided.

8. Source of Trust/Authority

Why should the core target audience trust this brand? What gives it authority? Why might we trust a cancer cure advertised by GSK, but not from a company we'd never heard from? Looking for firsts, superlatives, originals, famous names, awards, bragging rights, etc.

9. The Future

What must the brand anticipate in the future? What opportunities, issues and threats are coming down the pike that your Future Brand Essence needs to anticipate? Cultural and macro trends, the economy, technology, demography, industry trends, what the category leader is doing, etc.

10. Future Brand Essence

Introducing the concept of Future Brand Essence and sharing examples. Reviewing the Brand Mirror™. Extracting and distilling the desired DNA of the brand. Key criteria to be met. Why stealing is good. Strategies for gaining consensus and closure.

11. Brand Vision

What kind of world or state of affairs do we want to bring about? What is your boon for mankind? Self-serving visions to avoid. Why Brand Visions are typically out of reach.

12. Now what?

We now have a Future Brand Essence and a Brand Vision. Now what do we do with it? Areas typically affected by Brand Essence. Why it's important to limit the number of ideas you commit to and to assign teams to champion the top initiatives. Keeping the outcomes under wraps.

13. Future Brand Essence Alignment

Aligning employees, internal processes and external creative expressions with the Brand Strategy. The BrandSharing™ process. Importance of Naming the Beast™ and the Slaughter of the Sacred Cows™. Challenging communications partners with *The Passion Meter*.

14. Brand Reinforcement and Tracking

Use of Brand Conversations™ for internal reinforcement and CompanyPulse™ for internal tracking. Employee segmentation: Bystanders, Weak Links, Loose Cannons and Brand Champions. Involvement strategies to grow the Brand Champion segment. Creating a Brand Dashboard.

15. Summary: Quiz Time!

Appendices

1. Qualitative Research Tools for Brand Understanding
2. Synectics and Consensus Building
3. Workshop Icebreakers/Energizers
4. Puzzles
5. Answers to Chapter 15 Quiz
6. Answers to Puzzles

1

What is a Brand, Branding and Messaging?

Some common definitions. The power and financial value of brands. How does messaging differ from brands and branding? Emotional engagement and rational persuasion. Two dangerous words to watch: Strategy and positioning. Why Brand Essence is at the top of the brand totem pole.

What is a brand?

This is one of my favorite questions, mostly because it prompts such a range of responses.

Typical answers include:

• Company	• Graphic design
• Product or service	• Advertising
• Identity	• Logo
• Look, feel, tone of voice	• Tagline

The other reason it's one of my favorite questions is because it does not get asked enough, and clearly it should be – given the kinds of responses I usually get.

Brands are so important to the world economy today and get talked about every day, so it still amazes me that so many people – especially those who work with brands professionally – are unable to correctly define what a brand is.

1

But then again it's not that surprising given some of the definitions of a "brand" that exist.

The Marketing Science Institute, for example, believes a brand is:

> *"A mix of values both tangible and intangible, which are relevant to customers and which distinguish a company or product from its competition."*

A mix of values that are relevant and differentiated? Feels a bit loose to me.

Tim Ambler of the London Business School, on the other hand, wrote:

> *"A brand is the promise of a bundle of attributes that someone buys and that provides satisfaction. The attributes may be tangible or invisible, rational or emotional."*

Technically faultless of course, but a bit too academic for me, a tad chalk-dusty and not particularly inspiring.

The late Stephen King, of the WPP group, wrote something better:

> *"A product is something that is made in a factory; a brand is something that is bought by a customer. A product can be copied by a competitor; a brand is unique. A product can be quickly outdated; a successful brand is timeless."*

I like this because it speaks to what a strong brand can deliver and some of the benchmarks that define a brand's success. It still comes up short however in nailing down a concise, inspiring definition of a brand.

My own definition of a brand, coined many years ago, is as follows:

> *"A brand is a set of memories and expectations that exist in people's minds, a file card in a mental Rolodex accessed at a moment's notice."*

So imagine you're walking through a grocery store, and you come to the popcorn fixture.

You look at the different brands presented there such as Pop Secret, Orville Redenbacher and Act II, and what happens?

> Strong brands have the power to evoke strong memories simply at the mention of the brand's name.

Out pops the Rolodex in your mind containing memories and expectations for each of those brands, and perhaps you remember Orville Redenbacher as the sweet old guy who invented gourmet popping corn and perhaps that's what will influence your eventual choice.

Now think of the word Volvo.

Is there another word forming in your mind? Does that word begin with the letter S? Is that word "safety"?

Now think of the word Disney.

Is there a picture now forming in your mind? Does it have large black ears, or is it a certain magical fantasy fortress? As in Mickey Mouse or Cinderella's castle?

What this demonstrates is that strong brands have the power to evoke strong memories simply at the mention of the brand's name.

Another way of putting it is that brands that are strong enough can actually take control of some of the memory cells in your brain and stay there for as long as your brain continues to function.

What this also demonstrates, perhaps more importantly, is that brands do *not* live in products, logos, company headquarters or even marketing departments. They live instead in the hearts and minds of people – usually the brand owners' customers and other target audiences.

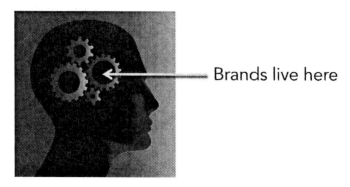

Brands live here

It also explains why strong brands are so important and so valuable.

Take a pair of regular sneakers, priced at $30. Present them branded as Nike and they can be sold at over $50. Branded as Gucci, perhaps double that amount. Why? Because of the memories and expectations (a.k.a. "perceived value") those brand names bring to a virtual commodity category such as sneakers.

Research data from the UK "session lager" beer category has shown, through "blind" and "branded" taste tests, well-developed beer brands performing poorly when tasted "blind" but performing very strongly when tasted "branded."

A great example of strong branding in the beer category actually overcoming drinkers' taste buds.

No wonder then that John Stuart, the former chairman of Quaker Foods, once wrote:

> *"If this business were to be split up, I would be glad to take the brands, trademarks and goodwill and you can have the bricks and mortar – and I would fare better than you."*

And look at the dollar value (a.k.a. brand equity) associated with the Coca-Cola brand: a whopping $71.86 billion as calculated by Interbrand in 2011. Not bad for a company that is essentially a giant marketing and licensing operation with all the production duties performed by licensed bottlers.

UK Session Lager: "Blind" vs. "Branded"

© 2013 BrandMechanics, Inc.

So let's say, for the sake of argument, the bricks and mortar in the Atlanta headquarters and offices around the world are worth $1 billion. That sum is still dwarfed by the dollar equity in the Coca-Cola brand itself.

And that's why it's increasingly common for owners of strong brands to put those brand equities on their balance sheets, making the company worth a lot more than its book value and making it much harder for a competitor to acquire it.

What is branding?

When I ask this question, the usual suspects arise again:

• Identity	• Tagline
• Look, feel, tone of voice	• Website
• Graphic design	• Image
• Advertising	• Packaging
• Logo	• Trade show booths

And this time, the answers are right – well, half-right really. The above incomplete list is actually some of the more traditional *external* expressions of branding – things that help express brands to the outside world.

There is however another, equally important side to that coin. And that is the *internal behaviors* of branding:

> **Having the external and internal aspects of branding in balance is crucial to success.**

- Customer service
- Crisis response
- Telephone manner
- Employee training, development and incentive awards
- Internal alignment of senior management and all other employees
- Vendor and strategic partner compliance/alignment
- Etc.

Having both the external and internal aspects of branding in balance and treating them both as crucial to the success of the brand is extremely important.

Imagine for a moment if "friendly" were a major part of your desired brand profile and you invested thousands or even millions of dollars creating a perception of "friendliness."

And then you hire someone as a customer service representative who has anger issues and gets irritable on the phone with customers who in turn blog and tweet about it to the world at large.

More damage gets done to your brand reputation with every customer service phone call (which, if you have an 800 number, you are actually paying for) because you forgot to align your external brand expressions with your internal brand behaviors.

The benefits of having an internal brand strategy go further than just avoiding obvious mistakes like the example quoted above however.

Strong brands typically:

- Attract better talent
- Have below average staff turnover, which saves on the "soft" costs of recruiting and training new personnel
- Build employee/partner pride, which translates into "ambassadors" for the brand
- Have lower customer acquisition costs.

So branding is more than just a logo or a label or other external expression of the brand; it's also a *principle* that can bring cohesion to an organization and help reinforce the brand and build it from within.

As many service companies will rightly claim, the best brands are built from within.

What is messaging?

It's estimated that the average individual is exposed to thousands – literally thousands – of messages every day. Broadcast media; digital media; products and their packaging in the home, out of home and on-shelf; logos on buildings, vehicles and apparel; hard copy journalism; the list goes on …

> Wherever there is a surface, there is a commercial opportunity for messaging.

Wherever there is a surface, there is a commercial opportunity for messaging.

Surely then, defining what messaging is should be pretty straightforward. But I regularly see confusion in client companies and their agencies (who really ought to know better).

And for the most part, the confusion is based on a lack of understanding of what a brand is and what messaging is.

The difference is essentially this: A brand is a set of memories that exist in people's minds. Messaging, on the other hand, is *what the brand owner is saying today.*

A brand is *more* than just communications.

It is a long-term benchmark that impacts:

- Business strategy
- Hiring
- Brand stretch opportunities

- Financial equity
- New product development
- Communications

Messaging on the other hand is about communications that need to be consistent with the brand:

- Advertising
- PR
- Online
- Packaging

- Promotions
- Events
- Trade shows
- Etc.

A quick example: BMW:

"The Ultimate Driving Machine" is BMW's famous tagline representing the BMW brand.

BMW's messaging however might vary from ad to ad, addressing the core values that underpin the brand: performance, build worthiness, technical innovation and luxury.

So while, for example, a performance message is a very different from a message about luxury, both are consistent with the brand as expressed by the tagline: "The Ultimate Driving Machine."

Take another example: BP:

For many years they have consistently built their brand as Beyond Petroleum, meaning they are a responsible energy company focused on the future.

During the Gulf Oil Spill crisis, it would not surprise me if the people responsible for their messaging had to come up with over 100 different messages to address the highly specific issues that must have arisen during that period. And the messaging likely changed frequently according to changing circumstances as the crisis unfolded.

If they were smart though, they would have ensured that each message was presented with a tone of voice consistent with a responsible energy company focused on the future.

What the above examples demonstrate then is that messaging can be short-term and tactical, quickly evolving according to changing circumstances.

The brand, on the other hand, should (if it has been crafted and managed properly) be a solid stake in the ground, a durable benchmark and guide for future brand development.

> Messaging can be short-term and tactical while a brand should be a durable benchmark.

Now back to messaging itself. I mentioned earlier the estimate that the average individual is exposed to thousands of messages every day.

But let's be clear, "exposed to" does not necessarily mean "listened to."

As George Bernard Shaw once said:

> *"The single biggest problem in communication is the illusion that it has taken place."*

So is there a "best practice" for communications and messaging to ensure you are understood?

There's certainly been a lot of discussion about it in the last 60 years with topics such as:

- USP (unique selling proposition)
- Single-minded proposition
- ESP (emotional selling proposition)
- Credo proposition (based on values or a manifesto)
- Differentiated proposition
- Brand messaging
- Messaging strategy
- Positioning statement
- Etc.

Rather than dissect all the above, let me simply put forward the guiding principles I believe in:

Messaging principle 1:

Single-minded messages work best.

In other words, saying one thing well is better than trying to say several things at once.

> Saying one thing well is better than trying to say several things at once.

Imagine I'm standing 10 feet away from you and throw you a tennis ball. There's a good chance you might catch it.

But now imagine instead that I throw you three balls all at once – there's a good chance you won't catch any of them.

Sounds simple? It should be. But there have still been many occasions in the past when a client has said: "Yes, but we've got a lot of other things we want to get across as well."

Thus begins an age-old ritual dance based on the client's desire to tell a complete story versus the agency's desire to present the most motivating aspect of the story that the target audience will want to reach in for.

Thus the line is drawn between the so-called "product-focused" versus "customer-focused" approaches to messaging.

Howard Gossage's famous quote points to the resolution of the debate:

> *"The real fact of the matter is that nobody reads ads. People read what interests them, and sometimes it's an ad."*

Although he is referring to print advertising, it still rings true for most forms of communication. Another way to put it: what's the point of spending money on a complete, detailed story if no one is interested?

Messaging principle 2:

Emotional engagement/involvement works harder than just rational benefits or product/service information.

Because if you have managed to engage/involve your audience, then you have succeeded in interesting them – you've given them something to reach in for.

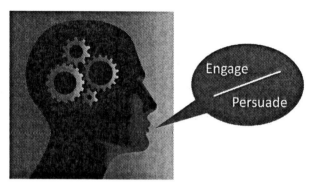

And let's not forget that there are whole categories of products which rely almost entirely on emotional engagement:

- Apparel
- Tobacco
- Alcoholic beverages
- Fragrances

Did you ever see an ad for Abercrombie & Fitch promoting the quality of their merchandise? Did Marlboro cigarettes ever discuss superior tobacco? Not that I recall.

What this shows is that brands can become very powerful without any rational product benefits whatsoever. Which is consistent with the view that emotional engagement works harder than just rational persuasion.

Another example, again from the UK, in the soap powder market of the 1980s and 90s:

Lever Brothers' *Persil*, the market leader, reputedly maintained a market share of twice that of Procter & Gamble's *Ariel*, its main competitor, and did so with roughly half Ariel's marketing budget. How was this possible?

Persil's brand essence, "Caring Whiteness," was consistently dramatized in TV spots with a mom's relationship with her son and making sure his white shirts were always clean. Always emotionally engaging, and rationally underpinned by whiteness.

Ariel's approach, on the other hand, might be summed up as "Provably Whiter." They took a rational, product comparison approach that supposedly appealed to the target audience's head rather than its heart.

And it consistently failed to make a dent in Persil's leadership, basically because it failed to engage its audience emotionally.

What is "strategy" and what is "positioning"?

I consider both these words to be potentially dangerous in the wrong hands.

Take the word "strategy."

On the one hand, a phrase such as "strategy development" can be enormously helpful as a shorthand for all things related to the thinking, research and planning work done in advance of the actual execution of, say, an ad campaign or a web design.

On the other hand, a big part of the problem is that "strategy" can also cover a multitude of sins and be used as a substitute for brand essence, or messaging or even positioning (more of which in a moment). Can "strategy" really equate to all those things?

> "Strategy" and "positioning" can be dangerous words in the wrong hands.

The ugly truth is that sometimes it does and many times it does not.

Another part of the problem is when the word is misused as in, for example, "Our strategy is to become the market leader."

Um ... sorry, that's not a strategy, that's an objective.

A better use of the word "strategy" in that instance would be an explanation of HOW that objective might be reached.

But then again, when I'm working with a team of professionals and we're being introduced to a new client and our leader says, "Tony will be responsible for creative; Mary will look after media; and Michael will take care of strategy" – I have to confess, I'm not going to complain because it makes things very simple for the client to process.

Now let's look at the word "positioning."

Fact is, it means different things to different people.

For some people "brand positioning" is interchangeable with "brand essence" – two to three words or a simple sentence to sum up the brand's DNA.

Others follow the more rigorous example, believed to have been originally established by Procter & Gamble, which takes the form of a template such as:

To [target audience], [brand name] is the [personality descriptor] [category noun] that [product benefit description].

So a (fictitious) P&G-style positioning statement might read:

"To moms of toddlers, Scrumptious is the happy candy bar that satisfies your child's appetite for longer."

I've also worked with design studios for which a "brand positioning" is nothing less than a highly detailed 3-5 page written document with a dozen or so sections to be completed.

So here we are in the world of brands and branding, where words have consequences, and there are at least three different interpretations of an important word like "positioning" according to whom you talk to.

> **Future Brand Essence sits at the top of the hierarchy of importance.**

My own approach is simple and highly practical: If a brand owner has a particular need in regards to positioning, then do whatever it takes to meet that need regardless of how "positioning" is defined.

And typically, that means developing a Brand Essence statement, or more accurately, a Future Brand Essence – defining what you *want* the brand to stand for in the future.

In the world of brands and branding, Future Brand Essence sits at the top of the hierarchy of importance because, when it is developed correctly, it will outlast all lesser components as a long-term benchmark for the brand.

Here is a simple summary of key brand strategy language:

Name	Definition	Role	Analogy
Future Brand Essence	The desired **DNA**, heart & soul of the brand – durable benchmark for what the brand wants to stand for.	Impact on business strategy, diversification, equity, vendor/employee relations, every customer contact, including all communications.	Desired **DNA** of a person.
Brand Positioning	Concise summary of the brand's core target audience and competitive leverage/difference today.	Drive differentiation through impact on communications.	Person's **appearance** in the market today.
Messaging	Focused, single-minded message for a communication.	Inspiration for the agency creative and media departments.	What the person is **saying** today.

© 2013 BrandMechanics, Inc.

One of the biggest questions that this table usually prompts is: so what is the difference between Future Brand Essence and Positioning?

The biggest difference is that a Future Brand Essence is a long-term benchmark, ideally underpinned by company values that will last at least five years or even twice that.

> A Future Brand Essence is a long-term benchmark, ideally underpinned by company values that will last at least five years or even twice that.

A positioning on the other hand can change and evolve according to who the target audience is, evolving market conditions, an improved product/service benefit and even what country you are in.

Take for example a maker of a widget, distributed through hardware stores, that drills holes faster than the competition. The brand essence might be "trusted friend." But the B2B positioning of "delivering more profit" won't be the same as the B2C positioning of "drills holes faster."

Now take a real-life example like McDonald's. In Hong Kong, the brand was positioned as a "value" brand in the QSR (quick-service restaurant) market. But back in the 1990s that was not going to work in mainland China where local QSRs were considerably less expensive compared to McDonald's. So the positioning had to change to something like "kids treat" or "convenient western food."

Lastly, consider another widget brand that positioned itself as the "fastest" and a new competitor enters the market with a product that is demonstrably twice as fast. Unless the first widget brand can come up with something faster, it will need to change its "fastest" positioning quickly or risk losing credibility.

Summary:

- A brand is a set of memories/expectations
- Branding is more than a logo – it's also an internal organizational principle
- Brands have power to overcome product deficiencies (UK beer example)
- Brands have financial equities worthy of inclusion on the balance sheet
- Messaging is what the brand owner is saying today
- Messaging works harder when it is single-minded and emotionally engaging
- Use words like "strategy" and "positioning" with care
- Brand Essence: At the top of the totem pole

Questions to ask yourself:

- What does *your* brand stand for?
- What do you *want* it to stand for?
- Is your brand's elevator pitch consistent, every time – or does it vary according to who is making the pitch and whom you are talking to?
- Imagine you are in mid-presentation in front a large group of people and a senior client asks you, "What exactly do you mean by strategy?" What exactly are you going to say?

2

The FBE™ Methodology —
Part 1: Logistics

Importance of advance logistical preparation. Calendaring issues and how to address them. Who should participate and why. Choosing the venue. Recommended equipment. What participants can expect.

At the conclusion of every Brand Workshop I have done over the past 15 years, the participants are typically both mentally exhausted and exhilarated at the same time.

Exhausted because the exercises are challenging both in content and in reaching a group consensus on each exercise's conclusion.

And exhilarated because, after about eight hours of creative problem-solving and consensus-driven decision making, the group has finally landed on two or three words or a simple sentence that nails down what they've been collectively struggling to nail down previously for weeks, months and sometimes years: An inspiring, memorable *desired essence* for their brand.

In the midst of all this mental exhaustion and exhilaration, I often get the reaction: "Wow – that was amazing – how on earth did you manage to do that?"

And when they say "that," what they are referring to is, in extreme cases, getting a boisterous, highly opinionated group of people (with egos ranging from big to the size of a minor planet) to agree on something widely believed by the group previously to be impossible to agree upon.

If I'm in a playful mood I might answer, "It's magic" or "It's all done with mirrors" or even "It's a trade secret – if I told you I'd have to kill you."

> To truly achieve focus, you have to make sacrifices.

The more serious answer is a broad combination of certain principles:

- Advance preparation, including calendaring the meeting, which is sometimes the hardest part of the whole process when busy senior executives are involved

- Pre-workshop exercises: Brand Audit (and, if possible, target audience research)

- Clearly structured workshop exercises, each with a beginning, middle and end

- Separate process facilitation from content generation

- Separate problem solving from decision making

- Ensure focus by requiring sacrifice and forcing choices

- Understand group dynamics and control the energy level of the group.

All the above may sound a little intimidating at first, even immobilizing. But, as with all seemingly large and complicated things, all we need to do is break it down into baby steps and everything falls into place and becomes much easier.

And that is the main purpose of this book.

Advance Preparation – Logistics

Calendaring:

Let's identify what is arguably the hardest part of the FBE™ process: calendaring the date for an offsite meeting of a group of people who are usually (or at least claim to be) extremely busy and who in many cases have been through some sort of "brand strategy" process before and found it either too dull, too frustrating, too much of a waste of time – or even all three.

Fortunately there is a relatively simple way of solving the scheduling problem.

Because it is fundamentally important to have the participation in the process of the most senior members of the group (e.g., CEO, CMO), begin the calendaring effort with their schedules.

> Once everyone else in the group realizes that the CEO and CMO are going to be attending the workshop, their schedules will magically open up.

Once everyone else in the group realizes that the CEO and CMO are going to be attending the workshop, their schedules will magically open up.

Basically, where their career ambitions go, their hearts will usually follow.

It also helps the calendaring effort to send a clear message to the group that their participation is crucial for defining the future of their brand, and by implication the future of their company or organization. This is a one-time deal that will have ramifications for the next 5-10 years.

One should never be as blunt as this, but the take-out from this message to participants should be clear: Don't complain later if you don't like the outcome of the workshop. This is an invitation to be part of a select, empowered team. Asking "How come …?" later on is not acceptable if you did not participate earlier in the "What if …?" part of the process.

In calendaring a Brand Workshop, always be sure there is enough time beforehand to conduct the Brand Audit and any customer research that may be necessary.

If for example, the process is just an internal Brand Audit and a Workshop, I typically can work to a two-week timeline: First week for Brand Audit input; second week for analysis and debrief preparation with the Workshop at the end of that week.

When customer or consumer research is needed, that may add another 4-6 weeks to the timeline.

Who should be invited to participate?

- Senior management, especially the CEO and CMO. Important for their inputs, their approval and, equally important, to give the process and outcomes authority and credibility.

- Others in the organization with strong opinions. Important to include these people especially if they are going to be potentially vocal and negative if they are excluded. Basically, ignore these people at your peril.

> Key participants are those who will make a difference both during the process and afterwards in championing and implementing the outcomes.

- Those best described as customer-facing – those whose work regularly brings them into contact with the organization's key target audiences. They will often bring unique customer insights to the process.

- Agency partners – representatives from design, advertising, digital and PR agencies that have an existing relationship with you.

- Overall: Those who will *make a difference* both during the process and afterwards in championing and implementing the outcomes.

One of the other questions that often arises at this stage of the planning is "What about people who say they can only attend for *part* of the workshop?"

My response is to discourage partial attendance because it can be potentially disruptive. If one participant declares they can come for only part of the workshop, what is to stop several others from doing the same thing?

Another way of looking at it is: What could be more important than spending one day defining the future direction of your organization for the next 10 years? Sitting at your desk pretending to be busy while texting your mom?

> Conducting a Brand Workshop via video link is certainly not ideal, but it can be done.

The only exception to this rule is when the CEO is constantly traveling or simply wants to make the point that they are so busy that they can only devote half a day. In that instance it's *essential* that they attend the afternoon session when the "heavy lifting" begins.

Another question I'm often asked is "Can we link in some participants via video conference?"

The answer to that is yes, but it's certainly not ideal. I've done this on several occasions and the downsides are:

- The process is slower, so you find yourself having to cut corners in order to keep to the schedule.

- The anonymity of the decision-making (more of which later) is compromised.

- If it's a single person linked in by video, they won't be able to take part in the team-based exercises, which not only can compromise their contributions but also leave them feeling left out and a tad frustrated – and the situation gets worse with multiple single participants taking part in this way.

In circumstances where certain people have to be part of the process and can only be linked in by video conference, it's better if there's a *group* being linked in so they can at least take part in the team exercises.

The last question, which has only arisen once, is "Can the Workshop include non-English speakers?" And the answer to that is yes. Back in 2011 I conducted an FBE™ Brand Workshop in China with some participants preferring to work in Mandarin. With a couple of translators, the workshop went off without a hitch.

Venue:

The ideal venue for a brand workshop is:

- Not in the office. Best to be away from desks, files, computers, phones, non-participating colleagues and all potential distractions and interruptions. Not having the workshop in your office demonstrates a commitment to dedicating the day to your brand.

- A room large enough for participants to work together around tables in groups of 4-6 people with still enough room for a computer projector, a projection screen and space for people to walk around freely if they want to.

- A place that is either close by to a catering facility or can actually take care of the catering arrangements itself. People will need to be fed and watered through the day, and it's one less task to worry about if someone else can take care of it. (I always recommend that breakfast should be served prior to the workshop kicking off as an incentive for participants to arrive promptly – and it usually works.)

- A space where there are inspiring views out of the windows. That means anything from spectacular natural scenery or cityscape to inside a zoo. The reasons for this are:

  o A great setting becomes part of the draw to get participants to attend.

o   It's also helpful in a very practical sense: When participants are struggling or mentally tired during one of the more demanding exercises, it's great to be able to walk to a window and stare out of it at something spectacular or arresting (whether it's a lush waterfall or a couple of alligators getting it on) and feel transported away from the problem-solving for a couple of minutes. You can then return to the task at hand feeling mentally refreshed and be able to take a new look at it.

(Needless to say, over my long career I've experienced both high and low points in this regard. High points include a lush setting in Penang, Malaysia, and a beautiful hillside retreat in Napa Valley; low points include a tiny hotel room with no windows and questionable ventilation, and a room with a boardroom table so big that participants could hardly move from their chairs.)

Couple of other things about the room:

- Best not to have any pictures, photos, art on the walls. By the end of the workshop, they will likely be covered with flip-chart paper, so the more bare wall space, the better.

- If the room has a large white or light-colored wall, great – you can project onto that wall and save yourself the trouble of finding a projection screen.

Equipment:

The amount of equipment will vary according to the number of participants.

- Computer projector

- Projection screen (not necessary if there is a white wall in the room)

- Electrical extension cord with 4-socket splitter (so you can operate the computer projector and power your laptop at the same time).

- Large 3M Post-It flip tcharts. Allow two for the moderator plus one for every five participants, so for a group of 10 you'll need four flip charts and for 15 you'll need five. Also be sure to avoid using non-adhesive flip charts – they require Scotch Tape which can damage walls.

- Flip chart easels for the flip charts (duh!)

- Black magic markers or felt-tip pens – broad-nibbed so writing can be seen from across the room. Enough for all the participants plus a few extra for the moderator.

- Letter-sized, lined writing pads and black pens for all

- A pack of 1,000 dark blue three-quarter inch round Color Coding Labels (sticky circular dots)

> Toys help participants relax and have fun, and as a result they generally have better ideas.

- Toys. I almost always bring toys to a Brand Workshop because they help participants relax and have fun, and as a result they generally have better ideas.

I usually bring Play-Doh, building bricks, bendy action figures, balloons, soft bats and balls, shuttlecock sets, bubbles, magic 8-balls, metal slinkies, etc.

Things to avoid: Toys that are noisy and projectiles that could cause injury.

What participants should expect:

In advance of the workshop, people will always ask, "So what's going to be happening at this workshop? What sort of questions are we going to be asked? And what time will we be finished?"

Reasonable questions. I find the best response is an agenda as follows:

7:30AM	Breakfast
8:00AM	Introductions, house rules
8:05AM	Brand Audit debrief presentation
8:30AM	Begin morning session
10:30AM	Coffee break
10:45AM	Morning session continues
12:30PM	Lunch
1:00PM	Afternoon session begins
2:30PM	Coffee break
2:45PM	Afternoon session continues
5:00PM	Wrap

In practice, the agenda has to be flexible. It makes no sense to cut off discussion in the middle of an exercise in which resolution appears to be minutes away.

Insist that there is no alcohol served at lunch as this will impair participants during the all-important afternoon sessions.

Summary:

- Logistical preparation in advance will help the process go smoothly
- Calendaring the Brand Workshop is half the battle
- Participation by senior stakeholders is crucial
- An inspiring venue is helpful for many reasons
- Get the right equipment
- Tell participants what to expect
- No alcohol at lunch!

3

The FBE™ Methodology —
Part 2: Tasks and Overview

Review of Brand Audits in general. The roles and importance of the internal and external Brand Audits. The importance of candor in the internal Audit. Key questions to be asked. Differences in approach for B2C and B2B external Audits. An overview of the FBE™ methodology and the Brand Mirror™.

So by now you'll have calendared the offsite, invited the appropriate participants, chosen a venue and you know what equipment you'll need.

But before embarking on the Brand Workshop, there are some key tasks to be completed: The Brand Audit and, when possible, Customer/Consumer Research.

Brand Audit

In its broadest sense, the term "Brand Audit" covers a multitude of sins – far too many to be realistic unless you have significant resources and time to devote to them:

- **Internal Brand Audit:** Input from senior stakeholders and employees.

- **External Brand Audit:** Input from customers, vendors, strategic partners, etc.

- **Communications Audit:** Review of all past and existing external brand expressions such as advertising, PR, packaging, promotions, point-of-purchase merchandizing, digital and social media campaigns, brand identity, web presence, trade shows, conferences, events, brochures, etc. Do the same for all internal brand expressions such as newsletters, new employee orientation programs, employee incentive programs, educational programs.

> **"Brand Audit" covers a multitude of sins – usually far too many to be realistic.**

- **Research Audit:** Review all past and current primary and secondary research studies.

- **Targeting Audit:** Review target audience segmentation – identifying and profiling the brand's existing and core prospective target customers.

- **Media Audit:** Review all past and existing traditional, digital, guerilla and experiential media strategies, budget allocations and spends.

- **Accountability Audit:** Review any marketing effectiveness, econometrics and ROI studies.

- **Press Audit:** Interview editors and journalists at relevant trade publications.

- **Product/Service Audit:** A.k.a. "product interrogation" – "interrogate the product until it confesses to its strengths."

- **Competitive Analysis:** Identifying, profiling, reviewing and comparing key competitors including their external brand expressions.

- **SWOT Analysis:** Review strengths, weaknesses, opportunities, threats.

- **Distribution Audit:** Review where and how the brand is currently distributed. Is it regional, national or global; is it bricks and mortar or just web presence; through mom & pops or national chains? Where are sales efforts focused?

Wow – such a long list.

Looks intimidating to the point of being immobilizing, and you could be forgiven for thinking this is way too much work to be done in preparation for a one-day brand workshop.

Fortunately, the reality is that in many cases you won't need to address even half of this list.

> The most common question about Brand Audits: "How quickly can we get this done?"

Sure, there are still large clients with large budgets that will want everything on this list addressed in complete detail. And depending on the level of detail required and the amount of data pre-existing, this would likely take three to six months and cost anywhere between $50,000 and $250,000.

But for most instances, this won't be necessary for three basic reasons:

- Not enough TIME. Back in the early 1990s it was still possible to allocate three to six months to developing a fully documented Brand Strategy. Twenty years later, everything has changed. Timelines have shortened, deadlines have become less negotiable, fees and timelines have been given greater scrutiny, and it's mostly driven by the need for faster turnarounds and a faster time to market. Cost obviously remains extremely important, but increasingly I'm finding the bigger question I face is: "How quickly can we get this done?"

- Not enough BUDGET. It's not uncommon these days to hear the plaintive cry of "I'm working twice as hard as I used to for only half the rewards." It's true for a lot of people – and that includes small and medium-sized clients as well as agencies, design studios and brand consultants. Clients are also more interested in flat-fee projects than open-ended customized approaches with hourly billing because they tend to have smaller overall budgets these days, they want more control over their budgets and they are increasingly more suspicious of firms billing by the hour or day without verification.

- Not enough BURNING DESIRE for a comprehensive Brand Audit. No self-respecting client wants to admit that they want to cut corners, but that's what happens in a lot of cases. Call it "cutting out the fat" or "cutting to the chase," but what it amounts to when budgets and timelines are tight is eliminating the majority of the components in the above list of Brand Audit activities.

Is there an element of risk in taking these shortcuts?

Of course, but that risk is substantially offset by focusing on those components that represent the best *value* in terms of time and money spent, and the sheer helpfulness and insight they bring to the Brand Workshop. And those two main components are:

- Internal Brand Audit (also referred to as simply the Brand Audit)

- External Brand Audit (also referred to as the External Customer Research)

Internal Brand Audit

Years ago when time was plentiful and budgets were sizable, the approach I took for the Internal Brand Audit was to interview key brand stakeholders in the organization with a topic guide customized specifically for that company.

In-person, internal Brand Audits are rigorous but also time-consuming and a money-maker for vendors.

This approach had, and continues to have, significant pluses and minuses.

On the "plus" side from a *vendor's* point of view, it's time-consuming and time is money so it's possible to charge fees for all sorts of things:

- Drafting the audit topic guide

- Submitting the audit topic guide for approval

- Taking feedback on the topic guide

- Amending the audit topic guide

- Resubmitting the audit topic guide and getting agreement

- Scheduling the audit interviews (say 12 one-hour interviews)

- Rescheduling some of the interviews – it's not unusual to have to reschedule the CEO interview a couple of times

- Executing the interviews – in theory this could be done in a matter of days, but in reality it can take a month

- Analysis of the findings

- Diagnosis and conclusions

- Drafting and finalizing the audit report

- Presenting the report

- All done, allow up to two months in total.

Of course there are still a lot of high-priced agencies, design studios and consulting firms out there who will argue that taking the time to conduct in-person interviews is the only right and proper way to do an internal audit. (After all, they have lots of support staff and office overhead to pay for, and this approach definitely helps with the bills.)

The "plus" from the client's point of view is that, in all fairness, this approach is arguably the most rigorous and most comprehensive way of conducting an internal Brand Audit.

So what about the minuses?

- Two months is too long and will be too expensive for many clients.

- The issue of candor: Can you be sure interviewees are being completely candid in their responses to your questions? Assurances of anonymity from the interviewer certainly help, but when it comes to tricky, internally political issues, will the interviewee have the courage to fess up? And if there are harsh criticisms in the audit report, will senior clients

> Faster, more efficient and candid beats time-consuming, more rigorous but potentially less candid.

put pressure on you to reveal who said what? (And trust me, this has happened several times although I continue not to cave in.)

So what to do?

After many years of conducting in-person internal Brand Audits with highly customized topic guides, I concluded that certain questions yielded better, more insightful results than others. And they worked across all categories, both B2C and B2B, NGOs, universities, start-ups and so on.

So the first step was to create a kind of questionnaire template which could be easily tweaked to customize it for the brand in question, have the questionnaire distributed to the Brand Audit participants and then ask them to send their responses back to me anonymously.

And as the participants were now working on their responses in their own time, I decided to add a two word-sorting exercises, named BrandAdvance™ (see below), which would not only generate candid insights into strengths, weaknesses and the desire for change, but also introduce the participants to the

> BrandAdvance™ exercises generate candid insights into strengths, weaknesses and the desire for change.

process of considering words carefully and making choices.

So now with a bit of simplification we can move from expensive, time-consuming, not-always-candid, in-person interviews (and by the way, word sorts in an in-person interview always seem to take forever) and have an approach that is faster, more efficient, less expensive and candid because of the anonymous responses.

The three exercises in the internal Brand Audit are as follows:

1. **BrandAdvance™ 1:** Sorting a list of "characteristics" (best to include a mix of both positive and negative words such as friendly, professional, imaginative, etc., as well as bureaucratic, internally political, slow, etc.) into one of three categories:

    o Existing but not desirable for the future

    o Existing and desirable for the future

    o Not currently existing, but desirable for the future

At BrandMechanics® we have lists of over 100 words to evaluate, so here are some of them to get you started:

* Ahead
* Authoritarian
* Bold/brave
* Bureaucratic
* Charismatic
* Clueless
* Disciplined
* Dull
* Esoteric
* Fearless
* Fun
* Hesitant
* Hip/cool
* Innovative
* Internally political
* Irreverent
* Kinetic
* Mature
* Mean spirited
* No balls
* Outspoken
* Overconfident
* Passionate
* Poorly managed
* Savvy/streetwise
* Stubborn
* Unadventurous
* Unfocused
* Unimaginative
* Upscale

When you've collected the responses from all the audit participants, the analysis will look something like this:

BrandAdvance™1: Characteristics

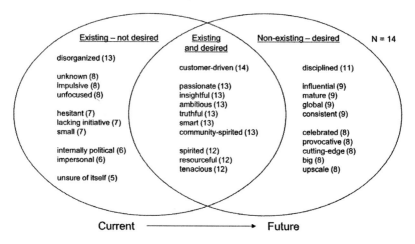

The left oval summarizes current internal perceptions of the brand, both good and bad.

The oval on the right however points to the future with a desire to hold onto the characteristics in the center and embrace those on the right which do not exist yet.

Interpreting these results can take time and practice and will always depend on the actual outcomes, but as a general rule this exercise will demonstrate an internal desire for change and improvement as evidenced by the contrast between the list of words on the left and the list on the right.

2. **BrandAdvance™ 2:** The second exercise in the recommended internal Brand Audit. This is another word sort similar to BrandAdvance™ 1 except that this time the words are "doing words." Again, it's best to include a mix of both positive and negative words such as inspiring, leading, enabling, etc., as well as drifting, juggling, complicating, etc.

And again the words get sorted into one of three categories:

- ° Existing but not desirable for the future
- ° Existing and desirable for the future
- ° Not currently existing, but desirable for the future

Again, at BrandMechanics® we have a long list of words, and here are some of them:

• Accelerating	• Lacking initiative
• Backsliding	• Liberating
• Breaking through	• Manipulating
• Catalyzing	• Monetizing
• Compromising	• Not communicating
• Connecting	• Nurturing
• Creating	• Pretending
• Developing	• Protecting
• Dithering	• Re-engineering
• Engaging	• Reversing
• Forcing	• Scaring
• Hiding	• Self-admiring
• Idling	• Stonewalling
• Improving	• Trendsetting
• Juggling	• Un-blocking

As with the previous exercise, the analysis will look something like this: (please see next page)

BrandAdvance™2: "Doing words"

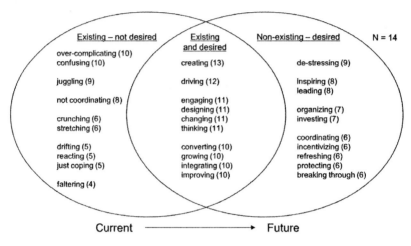

© 2013 BrandMechanics, Inc.

3. **Brand Audit questionnaire:** This is the third exercise in the recommended Internal Brand Audit. After years of experimenting, I concluded you only need about a dozen questions:

- **Target audience:** Who are the core target audiences, in rank order, you want to have a stronger relationship with?

- **Competition:** Who are your key competitors and why are they important?

- What are (or for start-ups, what are going to be) your key strengths? No need to be shy.

- Now turn it around: what are your key weaknesses? Candor is important here.

- **Part 1:** If this brand were an animal, what kind of animal would it be TODAY?

  Part 2: What sort of an animal would you like it to be in the FUTURE?

© 2013 BrandMechanics, Inc.

- **Part 1:** If this brand were a car or vehicle, what kind of car or vehicle would it be TODAY?

  Part 2: What sort of car or vehicle would you like it to be in the FUTURE?

- **Part 1:** If this brand were a beverage, what kind of beverage would it be TODAY?

  Part 2: What sort of a beverage would you like it to be in the FUTURE?

- What are the macro trends culturally/socially and specific trends within your brand's category that represent future opportunities and threats?

- Imagine it's six months from now and your brand is featured on the front page of *The Wall Street Journal.* What do you want the headline to say?

- What do you believe the main obstacles are to success within your organization?

- What main things within your organization do you believe should be preserved at all costs?

- **Part 1:** Write a "bumper sticker" (no more than five words) to advertise your brand as it is today.

  Part 2: Now write a "bumper sticker" (no more than five words) to advertise your brand as it will be in five years' time.

The kinds of responses you will get from these questions typically run from the completely banal to the brutally honest.

More importantly though, you'll get a good understanding of the key issues that people in the company agree on and disagree on.

And in addition, it is good practice for the workshop participants in compressing (a.k.a. headlining) their thoughts.

It's not unusual, for example, for the strengths in the company to be listed also under weaknesses. It could be the company's product or the company's founder or the business model or something else.

It's also not unusual for the list of strengths to be shorter than the list of weaknesses. This does not mean the weaknesses outweigh the strengths, but rather that there is generally greater consensus on the strengths and a long "tail" of little complaints on the list of weaknesses.

External Audit (Consumer/Customer Research)

Having identified and analyzed internal perceptions of the Brand through the Brand Audit, it's always a good idea to have external perceptions to compare them against.

This is important for a couple of reasons:

- Because a brand is a set of memories/expectations that reside in the minds of the target audiences, external perceptions carry a lot more weight than internal perceptions.

> The kinds of responses you will get from these questions typically run from the completely banal to the brutally honest.

- Which means the external perceptions become an important reality check against which the internal perceptions can be judged.

Sometimes the internal and external perceptions are broadly consistent, but on other occasions they won't be.

I've worked with many clients whose inflated perceptions of their product have been brought back to earth with a thud by their customers' candid comments.

I did some focus groups in Germany as part of a global project several years ago for an enterprise e-commerce software company. I was sitting behind the two-way mirror listening to the simultaneous translation with a senior client who was getting agitated that the respondents were not excited about his product and its game-changing possibilities.

His first instinct was to blame the moderator for not presenting the product appropriately and not asking the right questions, so I sent him into the group towards the end of the session so he could talk directly (he was a German, so there were no translation problems) to the respondents.

Poor guy. His presentation of the product and his questions made no difference, and the company switched as a result from an old-style product-driven strategy to a more customer-centric approach.

But on the other hand, I've also worked with clients who were surprised and delighted that their customers thought more highly of them than they themselves did, which gave them a lot more confidence moving forward, and they were able to build on assets they previously thought did not exist. Good result.

The actual form of the external brand audit customer research overall however does depend on, broadly speaking, whether the brand is B2C or B2B and on the scale of the Brand Strategy development project.

For example, back in 2002, I worked with Attik as their sole strategic planner to launch Scion – Toyota's Gen-Y-targeted range of cars, and the research efforts included focus groups, online surveys, video ethnography, cultural intelligence, video diaries, photo ethnography, street interviews and beeper ethnography.

> I've worked with many clients whose inflated perceptions of their product have been brought back to earth with a thud by their customers' candid comments.

But for smaller projects, focus groups or IDIs (in-depth interviews) are a reliable standby.

When focus groups are properly framed, recruited and moderated, they can be a powerful tool for the following reasons:

- Fast turnaround

- Relatively inexpensive (compared with large quantitative studies)

- Sensitive and diagnostic – meaning, for example, one comment from a participant can change the direction of the discussion and you can pursue it in a way that you can't with quantitative surveys, which are limited by the hypotheses incorporated into the questionnaire.

But focus groups often get a bad rap these days:

- Exploring attitudes and claimed (rather than actual) behaviors –

which is why ethnography has been increasing in popularity

- Inadequately trained moderators – some are not sufficiently skilled or experienced enough to spot when respondents are misrepresenting themselves, posturing or "following the herd," while others are so linear and wedded to the topic guide that they are reluctant to explore new hypotheses that arise during the course of the discussion

- Poor recruitment done by lazy recruiters who bring in regular focus group "professionals" instead of fresh respondents – including people who start talking about "positioning" and "targeting" or try to represent people other than themselves

The answer to these flaws is to ensure you have a trained, experienced moderator and find a recruiter you can trust.

As for focus group content in the case of an external Brand Audit, I broadly follow and expand on the topics outlined in the internal Brand Audit discussed earlier in this chapter to enable direct comparisons between the two audits.

Focus groups often get a bad rap these days.

Additionally there are a lot of different tools you can use, such as Brand Land, Brand on Trial, Brand Obituary, etc. that can be very helpful. (See full list of brand perception tools that I recommend and their descriptions in Appendix 1.)

B2B Brand Audits, in contrast to B2C, usually require a different approach.

While with B2C you need to gather perceptions from a representative sample of the brand's consumers from the general population, with B2B you need to talk directly with the brand's actual business customers.

And while it is sometimes possible to have actual customers come to a focus group with appropriately generous cash incentives, a much easier way is simply to arrange to speak to the customers over the phone for 30 minutes, which is typically the maximum amount of time they will commit to upfront.

At BrandMechanics® our CustomerPulse™ program consists of 12 half-hour interviews with our client's customers.

I always recommend a mix of "good" customers (to identify strengths) and "difficult" customers (to identify weaknesses).

Another good mix is 4 existing customers, 4 prospects and 4 lapsed customers.

Now B2B clients sometimes resist the idea of an independent third party talking directly and unsupervised to their customers. The client's customer relationship managers are often the most nervous.

This resistance can usually be overcome by being completely transparent with your client and emphasizing:

- It's important to get the unvarnished truth.

- No-one is going to be thrown under the bus if customers express dissatisfaction with individuals.

- Customers will be more willing to participate if the request is framed as asking a favor and expressing a desire to listen to their needs and opinions – because at the end of the day, people do like being asked their opinions.

The topic guide usually parallels the internal Brand Audit discussed earlier but needs to be shorter to reflect the fact that you have only 30 minutes.

> B2B Brand Audits, in contrast to B2C, usually require a different approach.

Some customers, particularly in the tech and financial services industries, often struggle with some of the more imaginative questions such as "If this brand were an animal, what would it be?" But with a bit of encouragement and patience, they'll come through with the information you need.

Methodology Overview

In the simplest terms, the core of the FBE™ Methodology is about populating the Brand Mirror™ below with highly compressed language to summarize the key aspects of the brand.

Each component represents an exercise that needs to be completed with the full participation of the brand's senior stakeholders working collaboratively to produce a concise summary of the particular aspect in question. And each component has an important role to play in defining the brand's narrative for the long term.

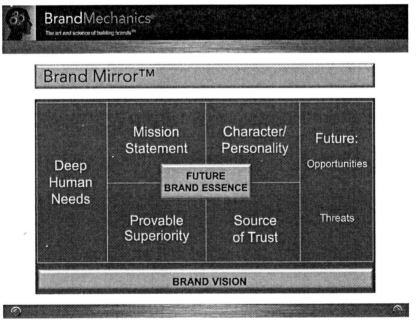

© 2013 BrandMechanics, Inc.

The individual components are as follows:

- **Mission:** The purpose of the brand. What the product, service or organization will *do* for its core audiences.

- **Provable Superiority:** What makes (or will make) your product, service or organization *provably* superior to its competition.

- **Deep Human Needs:** The deep human needs of your core target audience and which ones the brand can best fulfill.

- **Character/Personality:** A distillation of the five most important *desired* personality characteristics.

- **Source of Trust:** Why anyone should trust the brand – its source of authority.

- **The Future (Opportunities/Threats):** The key *macro/cultural/social* trends that could help or harm your brand in the future.

- **Future Brand Essence:** In 2-3 words or a simple sentence, what you *want* the brand to stand for in the long term.

- **Brand Vision:** The kind of world or state of affairs you *want* the brand to bring about.

Each one will be addressed in detail in the following chapters, together with step-by-step processes to achieve the rich, compelling, compressed language that is needed.

Summary:

- "Brand Audit" covers a multitude of sins – usually far too many to be realistic unless you have a couple of months and a significant budget.

- The key components of a realistic Brand Audit are an Internal Brand Audit (senior stakeholders and employees) and an External Brand Audit (focus groups typically for B2C and telephone interviews for B2B).

- The Brand Mirror™: A framework for building a cohesive Brand Strategy.

4

Mission Statement

Mission Statement and its purpose. How companies can get it wrong. What does the brand actually do for its core target audience? The roles of the brand, rational and emotional. The importance of choosing the right "doing words." Testing your Mission Statement.

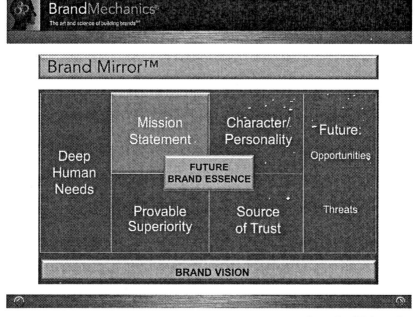

© 2013 BrandMechanics, Inc.

A Mission Statement is meant to define the purpose of a brand or company, what it is in business to do.

Problem is, many organizations interpret that, wrongly, as one of the following:

- Making money

- Becoming No. 1 in the industry

- Building shareholder value

- Crushing the competition

- Building the business and then selling out so we can all retire in comfort

- Etc.

Why are these so wrong?

Because they are all entirely selfish and display a complete disregard of the target audiences (consumers or customers) you're hoping will part with their money to purchase your products or services.

> **Avoid Mission Statements that are selfish and display a complete disregard of the target audiences.**

And they give no clue as to what business you are in.

As consumers continue increasingly to scrutinize the companies they buy from, which Mission Statement would you rather they read about as they search your website and the web in general?

(What follows is for a brilliant digital media services company I consulted with recently.)

A. *We will become the No.1 in digital media services globally.*

OR

B. *We will constantly discover data-driven consumer insights to create and accelerate performance across the entire digital ecosystem. We will open clients' eyes to ignite the potential of their people, brands and customer relationships.*

The differences between the two are striking:

Statement A is puffery and instantly forgettable. It makes no promises to their customers. It demonstrates no understanding of the needs and motivations of their core target audience. And it gives no guidance as to how that goal will be achieved.

Statement B, on the other hand, says exactly what they are going to do for their customers. They are going to *discover, create* and *accelerate.* They are going to *open eyes* and *ignite potential.*

In short, they are making powerful, motivating promises to their customers, and you get a clear impression of the kind of business they are in.

How did this come to be written?

By following the first major step in the FBE™ Process, a big part of which is choosing your "doing words" (in the above example, words like *discover, create* and *accelerate*) very carefully.

Because owning a "doing word" can be a powerful way of building a brand.

Who "owns" *driving* in the auto industry? BMW.

And who "owns" *thrive* in the healthcare industry? Kaiser Permanente.

In Chapter 3, we discussed the Brand Audit, and part of that was BrandAdvance™ 2 which sorted doing words into buckets. That exercise may give you some clues as to what you might consider using in your Mission Statement.

The principal step in the overall FBE™ Process however is to ask yourself the fundamental question:

What does the brand actually DO (or is going to DO) for its core audience?

What many years of doing brand workshops has shown me is that most companies can easily state what they *are* but find it much harder to describe in simple terms what they actually *do* for their audiences.

> **What does the Brand actually DO for its core audience?**

And here's the secret to successfully answering the question:

There are actually two complementary but distinct answers to the question.

The first is the *rational* answer; the second is the *emotional* answer.

Take washing machines as an example.

What do washing machines do?

They clean clothes, right? A sensible, entirely rational answer. But maybe there's an emotional answer as well, such as: They *reassure you that you're sending your kids to school in clean clothes.*

So already you have *cleaning* and *reassuring* as possible doing words for your Mission Statement.

Let's take another example: Digital cameras. What do they do rationally and emotionally?

Take photos and give you bragging rights about having a cool piece of tech to show off?

How about:

Rational:

> *Captures, stores and records images; and gives you flexibility and control, anywhere.*

Emotional:

> *Reflects your unique, artistic vision; and unleashes and satisfies your creativity.*

Again let's take a look at the doing words: *capture, store, record, reflect, unleash, satisfy.*

Words that start to build a picture, an impression of what the brand is all about, by describing what the brand can do for you.

Now a word of caution. Creating rational and emotional answers to the question "What does the brand do?" may seem simple at first, something that can be written in a couple of minutes, but it's not.

> The emotional answer to "What do you do?" is significantly harder than the rational one.

In the brand workshops I've conducted over the past 10 years, it's not been unusual for participants to take a couple of hours to nail down statements such as those above. It can take a lot of effort, collaboration and, most importantly, soul searching to come up with answers that are compressed, inspiring and durable.

Typically the emotional answer is significantly harder than the rational one, which is why as part of the brand workshop process I usually divide the group into smaller teams – one to address the rational question and the other to address the emotional. With larger groups I'll even ask two teams to address separately the emotional question with just one addressing the rational side of things, because the emotional answer is always tougher.

Avoid long, meandering sentences that try to include everything.

Weigh every word carefully and avoid ideas that are repetitive or contradictory.

And if by chance you come to a statement and you're not sure if it's rational or emotional, don't worry – it's probably both and that's not a bad thing.

The best test I know of for seeing whether your proposed Mission Statement "works" or not is to imagine you are being interviewed by a famous business journalist and they ask you, "So tell me, what exactly does your company/brand actually do for your customers?"

Then, in front of some trusted colleagues, say your Mission Statement out loud. Then ask them in all honesty if it sounds phony, or pretentious, or awkward, or too long, or pretty darn good?

Now with your Mission Statement done, you have completed the first exercise out of the eight required to define your brand strategy.

Summary:

- A Mission Statement defines the purpose of the brand/company.
- Avoid self-serving Mission Statements.
- State what you are going to do for your target audience, both rationally and emotionally.
- Keep it as short as possible.
- Choose your doing words carefully.
- Avoid repetition and contradiction.
- Always test your Mission Statement out loud and get reactions.

5

Deep Human Needs

What is a Deep Human Need, and which ones in the core target audience can the brand best fulfill? Using the Deep Human Needs approach as a surrogate for target audience needs especially when consumer research is not a viable option. A list of all the Deep Human Needs you'll probably ever need.

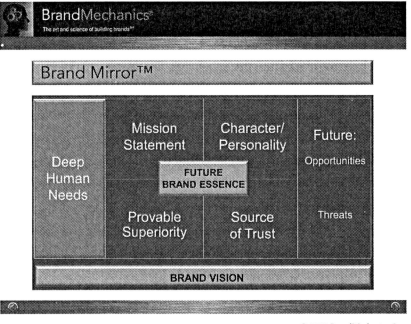

When I first started doing brand workshops, one of the significant challenges I faced was how to include the point of view of a brand's target audience in the development of a brand strategy when no audience research had been done.

After all, brands exist in people's heads, so isn't their input crucial?

The usual solution, doing consumer/customer research, would obviously be ideal, but it's also time-consuming, and expensive if you want to do it right. And there were clients out there with budgets that could not stretch to qualitative, let alone, quantitative research.

And then after a lot of thought around the subject, I had an "aha" moment:

> *Target audiences can tell you where your brand is today; they can't always tell you where it wants to go.*

Meaning:

> *Where your brand wants to go is up to you and your brand stakeholders.*

Or to quote Henry Ford:

> *"If I had asked people what they wanted, they would have said faster horses."*

Which is consistent with the view that brands should be built from the inside out, not the other way around.

Fine, but we can't ignore the target audience's needs and motivations entirely.

And that's when I had the idea of Deep Human Needs to address the challenge.

A single Deep Human Need can represent several consumer needs.

This is how it works: Imagine the brand is a car polish and you ask consumers why they bought it. They might respond:

- I need to protect my car.
- I need my car to look good before I sell it.

- I want to impress my spouse.
- I can't stand a dirty-looking car.
- I want to make my neighbors envious.

All legitimate consumer needs, and one could spend several thousand dollars on consumer research having them identified, analyzed and prioritized.

I would venture to say however that all five of these consumer needs are in fact rooted in a single Deep Human Need: Pride in one's possessions.

So what we've demonstrated is that a single Deep Human Need can represent *several* consumer needs (as consumers themselves express them), and can therefore act as a *surrogate* for them in the process of developing a brand strategy.

Having said that, the idea of Deep Human Needs does not make consumer research redundant – far from it. In an ideal world it's great to have masses of quantitative data covering your target's profile in terms of demography, geography, psychographics, behaviors and attitudes, and the sensitive, diagnostic insights best derived from qualitative research.

Without consumer research you can't segment your target to determine your core audience; and you can't get close to their rituals and the language they use in describing their interactions and relationship with your brand.

> Generate a short list of Deep Human Needs prioritized by how your brand can best fulfill them.

But in an increasingly time-crunched world of diminishing resources, the idea of Deep Human Needs represents a remarkably helpful and reasonable solution to the challenge of having your target audience's point of view included in the brand development process.

So how does it work in a Brand Workshop?

The goal is to generate a short list of Deep Human Needs prioritized according to which needs your brand can best fulfill, so let's break that down into baby steps.

Step 1: At this point, who do you believe is your core target audience? If you and/or your team have completed the Brand Audit described in Chapter 3, you should have a good working hypothesis as to who is most likely to want your product or services.

It's not necessary at this stage to define your core audience in huge amounts of detail.

Target audience definitions might be:

- Mothers of infants
- Investors
- CMOs and marketing executives
- IT directors
- Wineries
- Meth users

- F500 companies
- Beer drinkers
- Prospective university students
- Solar panel distributors
- Young adults
- Etc.

Step 2: Now generate a list of possible Deep Human Needs you believe your target audience has.

Here are some examples to get you started:

- Accountability
- Acknowledgement
- Approval
- Attention
- Authenticity
- Balance
- Belonging
- "Being ahead"
- Being understood
- Certainty

- Challenge
- Companionship
- Confidence
- Connection
- Consistency
- Control
- Collaboration
- Commitment
- Convenience
- Culture

- Currency
- Dignity
- Discovery
- Dreams
- Education/learning
- Escape
- Empowerment
- Entertainment
- Excitement
- Experimentation
- Expertise
- Flexibility
- Fun
- Gratification
- Growth
- Guidance
- Hope
- Ideas/innovation
- Independence
- Individuality
- Indulgence
- Influence
- Information
- Inspiration
- Interaction
- Joy
- Leadership
- Looking good
- Making a difference
- "Making it easy"
- New experiences
- No embarrassment
- Nurturing/nourishment
- Optimism
- Passion
- Partnership
- Perspective
- Prosperity
- Purpose
- Pleasure
- Pride in one's possessions
- Recreation
- Resources
- Safety/security
- Satisfaction
- Self-expression
- Self-improvement
- Shelter
- Simplicity
- Solutions
- Sophistication
- Spirituality
- Stability
- Starting over
- Staying ahead
- Stress relief
- Success
- Survival
- Relaxation
- Rescue
- Respect
- Responsiveness
- Risk-taking
- Reward
- Time out
- Transparency
- Validation
- Value
- Variety
- Vision
- "Wow"

What I continue to love about this exercise is that once people "get" it, they have no trouble in completing it – the brainstorming comes easily.

Step 3: You have your "long list"; now review it.

Are there any duplicates that need to be removed? In the above list for example, is the need for "acknowledgement" the same as the need for "respect"? And if so, which one should be removed?

Step 4: Your list is now de-duplicated; now it's time to prioritize it.

The question to ask yourself and your team is: Which of these Deep Human Needs can your product/service best fulfill? (So that we're clear, the prioritization is not to determine which Deep Human Need is most important to the target audience.)

For efficient prioritization within a group, I often use the technique of Power Dots. See Appendix 2 for more details.

> **Force choices to create debate and create consensus.**

Step 5: You have now a de-duplicated, prioritized long list of Deep Human Needs. Now let's cut off its tail to create your final short list.

If the list is five or fewer, well done. But usually it's longer than five, so I will typically propose taking the top five and discarding the rest. If objections are raised, discuss the importance of the ones being discarded and see if they deserve not to be cut.

One of the underlying strategies of the FBE™ Process is to force choices as a way of creating debate and gaining eventual consensus. It entails achieving focus by sacrificing the less important details, and the Deep Human Needs exercise is a good example of this.

Basically, it's very easy to generate a long list of things and think that the job is done. It's much harder, and much more useful, to create a prioritized short list that has been carefully considered.

Now before moving on to the next chapter, it's worth addressing an issue that sometimes comes up during this exercise: What if there is more than one core target audience?

Sometimes after much soul searching to see if one target audience is more important than another, the conclusion is that there are, for the sake of argument, two equally important and quite distinct target audiences. So what do we do?

The simple solution is to complete steps 1-3 for both target audiences and then compare the two long lists and see where they overlap.

From past experience, there will be overlap in most cases. So then take those that overlap and continue with steps 4 and 5. And in the unusual event that there is very little overlap between the two lists, keep them separate and continue with steps 4 and 5 for the lists individually. They will both then be included in the Brand Mirror™ towards the end of the process.

With your list of Deep Human Needs done, you've now completed the second of the eight exercises required to define your brand strategy. The Deep Human Needs will serve as a benchmark for the Future Brand Essence later in the process on the basis that a well-defined brand needs to fulfill at least one (ideally more than one) of the Deep Human Needs of your core target audience.

Summary:

- Deep Human Needs serve as a reasonable surrogate for target audience input, particularly when research is not a viable option.
- They can't however replace detailed quantitative and qualitative target audience research and cannot help you get close to audience segmentation, rituals, language, etc.
- Generate the initial long list, then de-duplicate and prioritize according to which needs your product/service can best fulfill.
- Cut the list to five if possible by sacrificing the less important needs.
- Constructive debate on the final prioritized short list is helpful.

6

Provable Superiority

What makes this brand's performance provably superior to its competitors? Rational benefits. The WCRS mantra for product interrogation. Why it's not always a good idea to accept the client's view that their product or service has no superiority.

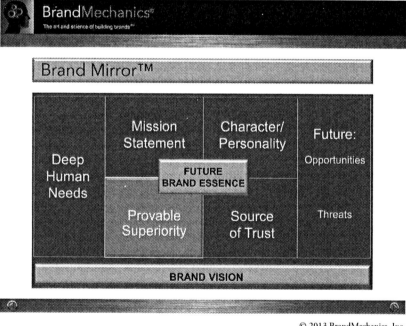

© 2013 BrandMechanics, Inc.

So what is it that makes your product or service superior to your competitors? And not just superior in your opinion and in the opinion of your team, but *provably* superior – something you could successfully prove in a court of law if you had to.

I've heard a lot of clients in the past tell me that their product is better than everyone else's. And many times, when I asked for proof to back up that claim, there's been a deafening silence. That's because many clients get caught up in their own excitement about a product or service and *want* it to be the best rather than having the evidence that proves it's the best.

And today, the concept of superiority is not limited to product/service performance. Companies and brands are increasingly being scrutinized for their values, ethics and transparency, as well as their social and environmental responsibility.

Who would have thought a few years ago that Apple would one day find itself under the microscope for its sweat labor supply chain? And remember the Nike scandal a few years back with child labor in Indonesia?

But let's say for the moment you can prove that your product is indeed the best. It does not necessarily mean however you can claim you have a superior product. Your product might indeed be the best, but if several of your competitors can match you in whatever it is that makes yours the "best," then you have a "top parity" claim, not a superiority claim.

It becomes the difference between "We're the best" (superiority) and "Nobody does it better" (top parity), which is a common, weasel way of sounding superior even if you are not.

Superiority can also be transient or time limited.

It was said a few years ago that if you launched a high-tech product that was superior to everything else, you had about six months before your competitor caught up with you. Today that lead time is often shorter and continues to get shorter.

> "Nobody does it better" is a weasel way of sounding superior.

Competitors copying innovators has been a fact of life for many years and has led to what some people call "design convergence." Ever noticed how similar cars look these days? That's an example of design convergence in action. But the principle applies across most industries from laundry detergent to golf clubs.

Another issue is the question: "Do I really need provable superiority to build a successful brand?"

And my answer to that is, "Not always." There are categories such as alcoholic beverages, apparel, tobacco, fragrances and luxury goods that have thrived for many years without superiority claims.

And there are other categories, such as technology where superiority is measured in such a complicated way that it makes no difference to the target audience, and commodity products with absolute product parity, so why bother?

What I'm leading up to is this: Provable superiority that will endure is hard to come by, so don't feel bad if you find yourself struggling to pin something down.

On the other hand, you do need to have something to say when you are inevitably asked, "So what makes your product/service better than the rest?"

> **"Headlining" means having to compress your thoughts.**

(And by the way, if you think that being "green" represents superiority these days, forget it. Too many companies have been "green-washing" themselves (i.e., pretending to be green) and have been called out as phony. Being green is expected these days.)

Assuming you don't have a cure for cancer or a widget that works faster than any other, examples might include:

- Product preference research

- Performance guarantee

- Patents

- Culture, people, standards, values

- Unique brand icon or persona (e.g., Mickey Mouse)

- Repeat-customer and/or client retention rates

- "Secret sauce" – an intriguing secret formula with a name, but you can't reveal the details behind it – think Chevron with Techron

- Size: smaller (more nimble/responsive versus lumbering competitors) or larger (which implies you must be doing something right).

So let's get down to what needs to happen in a group or workshop environment.

Step 1: Create a list of points of superiority. The list needs to be "bullet point headlines" – short and to the point.

If someone in the group makes a long speech about a particular point of superiority, that's great but then ask, "What's the headline?" This is important because long speeches can be a pain to capture. Asking for the "headline" is a great way of requiring the speaker to compress their thoughts into something that summarizes the point in an easily understood way.

No need for the points to be "provable" at this stage as this may shut the discussion down too quickly. Better to capture as many bullet points as possible, no matter how wild they might sound.

Step 2: You have a bullet point list of candidate superiority claims.

Now examine each claim in turn and see if it can be verified (defended in a court of law) and/or needs to be tightened up or qualified somehow (e.g., if you can't say you are the fastest in the industry as a whole, could you say you are the fastest in a category within the industry?)

Step 3: You now have a "bullet-proof" list of superiority claims.

Now prioritize them in rank order on the basis of how strong a case each point makes regarding your product/service's superiority. (Easiest way to do this in a group is Power Dots – see Appendix 2 for more details.)

With your list of Provable Superiority done, you've now completed the third of the eight exercises required to define your brand strategy. Provable Superiority provides the opportunity for differentiating your brand on a rational basis particularly if you favor P&G-style positioning statements.

One last thing though.

From an agency/design studio/ consultancy's perspective, it's usually a reasonable assumption that a client will be fully aware of their product's superiority.

Clients are not always aware of their product's strengths.

And that can sometimes be a false assumption and highlights the importance of doing a proper product interrogation.

When I was working at WCRS in London in the 1980s, we were pitching 3M's Scotch blank videocassette business.

The client told us their product had no superiority; it was a parity product languishing at No. 5 in the market.

But being WCRS, Robin Wight's famous mantra "Interrogate the product until it confesses to its strengths" applied, so I traveled to 3M's manufacturing facility in Gorseinon, South Wales, and interviewed the top technologists there.

It soon became clear that there was a significant product difference. 3M's expertise in surface technology had led the company to put a textured graphite coating on the back of the polyester tape that had the recording surface on the front.

This "back coating" had *four* distinct advantages:

- By being textured (under a microscope it looked like a plowed field), it ensured a straighter journey through the video recorder's tape head for better tracking.

- It's made of graphite, like the "lead" in a pencil, which is a lubricant so the tape had a smoother journey through the tape head.

- Graphite is also an electrical conductor, so it eliminated any potential build-up of static charge.

- Most important of all, when the tape was wound up tight in the cassette, the back coating acted as a soft cushion against the delicate recording surface and so minimized any disturbance of the surface which can cause the "white snow" effect on a TV screen when playing an over-used videocassette.

With a protected recording surface, it meant you could re-record over and over again without any significant negative impact on the quality of the signal being recorded.

The technologists then showed me the results of the tests they had conducted which indicated that after 500 re-records on the same tape, there had been no significant deterioration of the signal.

Later, we asked them to repeat the test with 5,000 re-records. And again there was no noticeable decline in the recorded signal quality.

> With a protected recording surface, you could record over and over again.

This then led to the famous "Lifetime Guarantee" (lifetime of the purchaser, not the product) and the Scotch Skeleton advertising which took the brand from No. 5 in the market to undisputed leader in less than 12 months.

I named the skeleton "Archie" – and the name stuck.

The point is however: None of this would have happened if we had simply accepted the client's view that the product had no advantages over the competition.

Summary:

- If product/service superiority is going to be an important part of your Brand Strategy, avoid being frothy and make sure it's provable – defensible in a court of law if necessary.

- Superiority is more than just product/service performance these days; it also includes company values, supply chain ethics, and social and environmental responsibility – your faster widget will count for squat if it's manufactured by anything halfway resembling a facility employing slave labor.

- Top parity is not the same as superiority.

- Durable superiority is increasingly rare in an arena of copying and design/product convergence.

7

Character/Personality

Why should the core target audience like this brand? Why character/personality is an important benchmark for all brand consistency and fundamental in categories like apparel, alcohol, fragrances and tobacco. A list of useful words and phrases. Words that are best avoided.

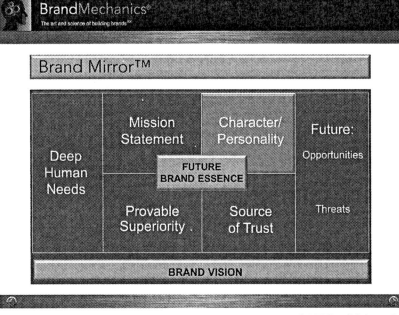

© 2013 BrandMechanics, Inc.

Why should your core target audience like your brand?

The concept of likeability is important and is often discussed in two separate but connected areas.

The first area is salesmanship. The idea is that in a store for example selling shoes, people are more likely to buy from a person they like. Absolutely true, and any good salesperson will confirm that.

The second area is advertising, which more often than not is trying to sell something. Back in 1991, the Advertising Research Foundation (ARF) published research that suggested, out of all the measures that can be attributed to advertising, likeability was the most likely to build brand preference and deliver advertising effectiveness.

Now to achieve the goal of being likeable, you need to define your brand's character/personality and then stay true to it consistently internally and externally, which means on every occasion your brand touches your target audience – advertising, online, packaging, PR, customer service, etc.

Maybe this sounds obvious, but it's not.

Imagine you have a brand and you want to consistently present it as "friendly" and you spend millions of dollars promoting your brand as "friendly."

> In some industries, your defined character/personality will be your ultimate leverage.

Then one day someone calls your customer service department with a complaint and your representative on the line is having a bad day, or the previous night had a row with their significant other, or they happen to be a sociopath who told lies to get their job. And they end up having a row on the phone which is not exactly "friendly."

The dissatisfied customer then tells all their friends about how *unfriendly* the experience was and blogs to vent about it and starts a Facebook community demanding an apology.

And all your millions of dollars of investment slowly starts to unravel …

Now imagine having a brand that you want to promote as "easy to deal with," and again, you spend millions of dollars promoting your brand as "easy to deal with." You establish an 800 telephone number for people to sign up, but when they do they hear a ghastly voice machine and it seems like an eternity before the appropriate option is spoken.

This time your millions of dollars have been undermined, and you even paid for the phone call.

So character is an important benchmark for the sake of consistency.

And perhaps even more importantly, for industries like alcoholic beverages, fashion, tobacco, luxury goods and fragrances, your defined character/personality is your ultimate leverage for building a powerful brand – think most vodka brands, Ralph Lauren and Marlboro.

So how do we go about defining a brand's personality?

First we need to embrace five common-sense rules:

1. Avoid long lists of personality characteristics.

    Long lists are useless because being long they are unfocused and lack specific guidance. It's easy to have a group come up with their favorite descriptors and everyone feels happy because their particular word or phrase has been included.

    But that list won't serve as any sort of benchmark when evaluating creative brand expressions because it'll be too loose.

2. Avoid "corporate" characteristics.

    Descriptors such as "successful," "global," "profitable" should be avoided because they are not personal.

    Have you ever met a person and remarked later that they had a "global" personality?

Try thinking of how you would describe your brand in terms of it being a person and you'll be on the right track.

3. Some descriptors must be *earned* rather than *assumed.*

   I always recommend avoiding descriptors such as "trustworthy" and "respected" because, while they are legitimate words for describing a person, trust and respect are attributes that have to be earned rather than simply adopted as part of a character/personality definition.

   Better to ask instead, what are the personality descriptors that, if pursued consistently, will lead to trust and respect.

   Another word I try to avoid is "honest." While it may be absolutely true, the use of it can also lead to a lot of unnecessary questions about honesty that are better left unasked.

4. Avoid the commonplace and obvious.

   Three words that almost always arise in this exercise are:

   o Passionate

   o Visionary

   o Innovative

   And I advise caution because of so *many* brands I've worked with wanting to be perceived in this way. I don't mean to imply these words should never be used – far from it. Just be sure you can justify them if asked.

5. Phrases work just as well as words, sometimes even better.

   Descriptors are powerful ways to define a brand's character/personality, and single words have the advantage of being simple to remember.

   But don't shy away from phrases. They can sometimes give greater nuance to the kind of personal characteristic you are trying to describe.

For example, instead of "committed," you might want to choose "whatever it takes" to create a mental picture of unwavering commitment.

So how do we get to a definition of your brand's character/personality?

Step 1: Ask your team to work individually and without discussion to think of a person they like and admire.

> Don't shy away from phrases – they can give extra nuance.

We don't need to know who the person is.

The person could be someone alive or an historical figure, someone you know very well or someone you'd like to meet someday.

So the person you like/admire could be your mother or Abraham Lincoln; each person needs to simply focus on their own chosen person.

Step 2: Now ask each member of the team to write down 10 words or phrases that describe the character/personality of that person.

Here are some that have arisen in over 70 workshops in the past 15 years:

- Accountable/results oriented
- Addictive
- Adorable
- Adult
- Adventurous
- Ahead of the curve
- Always delivers
- Ambitious
- Anticipator
- Approachable
- Assertive
- Authentic
- Balanced
- Beautiful
- Big hearted
- Bold
- Brilliant
- Calmly determined
- Can do
- Caring
- Centered
- Challenging
- Charismatic
- Charming
- Cheeky
- Chill

- Classy
- Collaborative
- Community spirited
- Compassionate
- Consistent
- Contemporary
- Cool/hip
- Courageous
- Creative
- Cute/cuddly
- Daredevil
- Democratic
- Demonstrative
- Detail-oriented
- Discerning
- Disciplined
- Disruptive
- Driven
- Dynamic
- Eccentric
- Eclectic
- Energetic
- Engaging
- Enthusiastic
- Epic
- Ethical
- Empathetic
- Empowering
- Enchanting
- Entertaining
- Entrepreneurial
- Evangelical
- Exhilarating
- Exotic
- Expert
- Extreme
- Eye-opening
- Fearless
- Fiercely competitive
- Fire in the belly
- Flexible
- Focused
- Fresh
- Friendly
- Fun to be with
- Game changer
- Geeky
- Generous
- Genuine
- Giant killer
- Going the extra mile
- Good listener
- Good natured
- Go-to person
- Grown up
- Gutsy
- Humble
- Imaginative
- Incisive
- Incomparable
- Independent
- Individualistic
- Influencer
- Innocent/child-like
- Innovative/inventive
- Inquisitive
- Insightful
- Inspiring
- Intellectually curious
- Intuitive
- Irreverent
- Knowledgeable

- Leader
- Legendary
- Liberating
- Likeable
- Magical
- Majestic
- Maverick
- Mesmerizing
- Motivating
- Neighborly
- Neutral
- Newsworthy
- Nimble/agile
- No nonsense
- Nurturing
- Open book
- Open-minded
- Optimistic
- Over the top
- Partners
- Passionate
- Patient
- Penetrating
- People's champion
- Pioneer spirit
- Playful
- Powerful, commanding
- Pragmatic
- Proactive
- Professional
- Progressive
- Provocative
- Pure
- Pushing the limits
- Quietly arrogant
- Quietly confident

- Quirky
- Reliable/dependable
- Resourceful
- Respectful
- Responsible
- Responsive
- Revolutionary
- Risk taker
- Rock solid
- Rugged
- Savvy
- Sensual/sleek
- Sexy
- Social/outgoing
- Sophisticated
- Spellbinding
- Spirited
- Spiritual
- Storied
- Storyteller

> Asking for "unusual" personality/character words stretches participants' imagination.

- Straightforward
- Stylish
- Supportive
- Surprising/astonishing
- Team player
- Tenacious
- Tireless

- Trailblazer
- Tribal
- Unapologetic
- Un-bureaucratic
- Uncomplicated
- Uncompromising
- Uncontainable
- Unconventional
- Understated
- Unwavering
- Vibrant

- Visionary
- Versatile
- Warm
- Welcoming/hospitable
- Whatever it takes
- Wholesome
- Wired/insightful/plugged in
- With integrity
- Witty
- Worldly
- Young at heart

Step 3: When they are done, it's time to share the results by having each team member write their 10 words/phrases on a flip chart or whiteboard. So if there are six team members, you should now have 60 words visible for everyone to see.

Step 4: Now ask your team, again working individually and without discussion, to write down just *five* words or phrases to sum up the *desired* character/personality of your brand.

If they want to use any of the words/phrases on the flip chart, that's fine. If they want to come up with completely new words/phrases, that's also fine.

I also always ask people to include at least one "unusual" word – and they can define "unusual" however they wish. This is important in getting participants to stretch their imagination and generate ideas that others can build off of.

Step 5: We must now capture, again on a flip chart or whiteboard, the words/phrases that have been generated.

Using the example of six team members, there will be a total of 30 words this time, but some may be duplicates. So capture each person's words one at a time, and leave out any repeated words.

You might now have around 20 words to work with.

Step 6: Some of the words may overlap, e.g., "smart," "intelligent" and "savvy." You don't want all three in the list, so discuss/debate which word or phrase the team prefers and strike out the others.

Step 7: Time now to prioritize the list. Power-Dot the list (see Appendix 2 for details), five dots per team member and lose any words/phrases that score two dots or less.

Step 8: Now comes the interesting part. The goal is to have no more than five words/phrases that sum up the desired character/personality of your brand.

How does this list that you've just generated stack up?

Ask yourself the following questions:

- Are all the words/phrases personal? Remember to strike out "corporate" words such as "global," "successful," etc.

- Have you avoided characteristics that are *earned*, such as "trusted"?

- Do any of them overlap – like "smart," "intelligent," "savvy"? De-duplicate as necessary.

- Are any of the items contradictory? Resolve any contradictions as needed.

- Are there more than five words/phrases? If there are more than five, which ones need to go?

- Remember to resist the temptation to allow more than five; allow it and the process of achieving focus through sacrifice will be undermined and your final list will be less useful.

> Debating which words and phrases should stay and which ones should go is an important step towards group consensus.

- Debating which words and phrases should stay and which ones should go is an important, collaborative step towards group consensus and commitment.

- Does the list excite you? If there are some dull words, strike them out and go back to some of the earlier lists and see if something more interesting has been overlooked and needs to be included.

- And be sure to check out the "unusual" words that the team was asked to generate and see if anyone wants to "champion" them.

- Read your list again. Are these the kind of qualities you would look for in someone you were going to hire in the future?

Step 9: With your final list of five that's been debated and amended several times, it's always worth re-prioritizing the list with Power Dots one last time.

Some examples of desired character/personality summaries:

A Las Vegas resort:

- Exotic
- Eclectic
- Adventurous
- Storyteller
- Chill

A digital media services company:

- Eye-opening
- Unconventional
- Geeky
- Tenacious
- Pragmatic

A sales consulting firm:

- Over-achiever
- Charming
- Big-hearted
- Energetic
- Whatever it takes

A famous beer brand:

- Charismatic
- Risk-taking
- Independent
- Confident
- Genuine

A new social media platform:

- Innovative
- Savvy
- Passionate/energetic
- Collaborative
- Proactive

A new town:

- Beautiful
- Vibrant
- Neighborly
- Fun/creative
- Engaging

A Las Vegas attraction:

- Great storyteller
- Provocative
- Visionary/innovative
- Generous
- Playful

A famous smart credit card:

- Agile/versatile
- Liberating
- Innovative/visionary
- Empowering/powerful
- Intelligent

A Napa Valley winery:

- Storied
- Rock solid
- Rugged/pioneer spirit
- Driven
- Enchanting

A project-sharing software firm:

- Fire in the belly
- Irreverent
- Friendly
- Smart
- Confident

A political coalition:

- Trailblazing
- Entrepreneurial
- Collaborative
- Sexy
- Vibrant

An established Catholic university:

- Brilliant/vibrant
- Provocative
- Visionary
- Creative/innovative
- Compassionate

A children's website:

- Fun
- Cool
- Adventurous
- Nurturing
- Dependable/safe

An iconic videogame character:

- Independent
- Sexy
- Adventurous
- Worldly
- Intelligent

With your Desired Character/Personality done, you've now completed the fourth of the eight exercises required to define your Brand Strategy. Character/personality is not only an important benchmark for your brand's look/feel and tone of voice; it also helps define the kind of people you may want to recruit in the future.

Summary:

- Likeability is a highly important aspect of brands and communications, hence the importance of a well-defined brand character/personality.

- It's a key benchmark for ensuring consistency of look/feel and tone of voice.

- Fundamental for those categories that tend to lack rational benefits such as alcoholic beverages, fashion, tobacco, fragrances, etc.

- Define your *desired* personality, not something that's existing.

- Create a list of five words or phrases.

- Common mistakes: long lists, corporate words, "earned" words, obvious words like "passionate."

- Phrases (not just words) are encouraged.

- Useful in recruiting future employees.

8

Source of Trust

Why should the core target audience trust this brand? What gives it authority? Why might we trust a cancer cure advertised by GSK, but not from a company we'd never heard of? Looking for firsts, superlatives, originals, famous names, awards, bragging rights, etc.

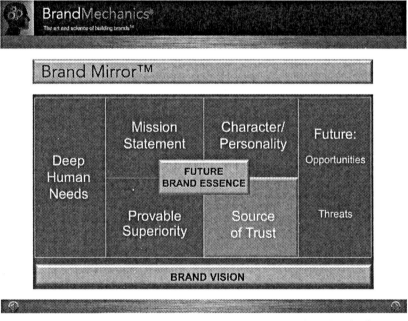

© 2013 BrandMechanics, Inc.

What gives your brand authority?

Or, put more bluntly, why should anyone trust your brand and anything you say about it?

As brands continue to be scrutinized by an increasingly skeptical public, it's important to have a clear and incontrovertible statement of provenance, track record, achievements and accolades in the public domain. And as with the Provable Superiority exercise, all the statements should be defensible in a court of law.

Basically, a brand needs credibility to be taken seriously.

For example, why might we trust a cancer cure advertised by a major pharma company but be more skeptical if the claim came from a company we'd never heard from?

The answer is simply that we are more likely to trust a brand we know (or at least think we know) than a brand we don't know anything about or enough about.

So let's start by asking some tough questions:

- Can you claim any superlatives? E.g., are you recognized as being the *first* or the *original* in the market, or *No. 1* in your category, or having the *fastest* growth rate, or the *widest* range of products/ services, or the *highest* customer loyalty rate, or the *lowest* staff turnover, etc.?

- Being able to claim and substantiate a superlative helps build credibility, even if you have to qualify it with "in the past five years" or "in the *organic* sector of the yogurt market" or "in the *luxury* car market."

- And if the superlative is just out of reach, there's no harm in settling for being No. 2 or No. 3 if the context warrants it.

- Hard numbers (e.g., sales exceeded $10 million in the first year) work harder than vacuous claims like "highly successful in the first year."

- Can you name-drop? E.g., marquee clients, backed by a high-profile venture capital firm, executives that formerly worked at famous companies, industry titans on your board of advisors.

It may sound like basking in the reflected glory of famous people and/or companies, but famous names *do* get attention and help build credibility.

> If a superlative is just out of reach, being No. 2 or No. 3 is fine if the context warrants it.

- Any other bragging rights? E.g., industry awards, tributes or positive commentary in the national or industry media or from iconic bloggers.

So on to the specifics:

Step 1: Create a list of points that will constitute your sources of trust. The list needs to be "bullet point headlines" – short and to the point.

If someone in the group makes a long speech about a particular point, that's OK but then ask, "What's the headline?" This is important because long speeches can be a pain to capture. Asking for the "headline" is a great way of requiring the speaker to compress their thoughts into something that summarizes the point in an easily understood way.

No need for the points to be "provable" at this stage as this may shut the discussion down too quickly. Better to capture as many bullet points as possible, no matter how wild they might sound.

Step 2: You have a bullet point list of candidates.

Now examine each claim in turn and see if it can be verified (defended in a court of law) and/or needs to be tightened up or qualified somehow (e.g., if you can't say you are the fastest in the industry as a whole, could you say you are the fastest in a category within the industry?)

Step 3: You now a "bulletproof" list of Source of Trust claims.

Now prioritize them in rank order on the basis of how powerful each statement is in establishing your brand's credibility. (Easiest way to do this in a group is Power Dots – see Appendix 2 for more details.)

It's not unusual to see overlap between Source of Trust and Provable Superiority, and if this happens that's fine because what you are most proud of might also be your most important benefit.

Which raises another issue: I'm often asked, "What is the real difference between Source of Trust and Provable Superiority?" Essentially, Provable Superiority is about what is *current*, what makes your product/ service better than the competition, what your core audience will find

> Prioritize your Source of Trust bullets according to how well they establish your credibility.

attractive and compelling. Source of Trust, on the other hand, is more about the *past*, your track record, what your core audiences will find *credible*.

Now with your Source of Trust done, you've now completed the fifth of the eight exercises required to define your Brand Strategy.

Source of Trust gives your brand a solid rational basis for credibility and is often leveraged in company annual reports and in the final paragraph of a press release to establish authority.

Summary:

- Source of Trust summarizes why your brand is credible and why anything you say about it can be trusted.
- Identify superlatives, brag with famous names, and look for tributes and positive commentary in the media.
- Hard numbers enhance credibility.
- Brainstorm your headlines as bullet points – don't try to capture long speeches – then verify and prioritize them.
- There may be overlap between Source of Trust and Provable Superiority.
- Leverage in company annual reports and press releases.

9

The Future

What must the brand anticipate in the future? What opportunities, issues and threats are coming down the pike that your Future Brand Essence needs to anticipate? Cultural and macro trends, the economy, technology, demography, industry trends, what the category leader is doing, etc.

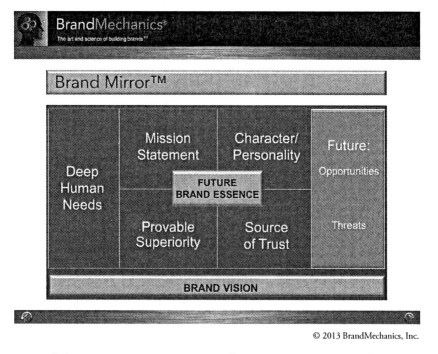

© 2013 BrandMechanics, Inc.

One of the most important aspects of writing a Future Brand Essence statement is that it should be durable. It's not going to be of much use if it becomes out of date quickly.

When I work with clients to develop their brand's desired DNA, I always have it in mind that we need something that will last five to 10 years.

So doing some crystal ball-gazing can be helpful in ensuring your Future Brand Essence will stand the test of time.

That's one of the reasons why I call the statement a *Future* Brand Essence, something that will continue to be relevant in the future. (The other reason, discussed in more detail in the next chapter, is that the statement should reflect what you want the brand to stand for in the future, not just what it stands for today.)

> Sort the key cultural and macro trends into opportunities and threats.

When trying to imagine the future, you might find it useful to think about the "usual suspects" in terms of cultural and macro trends and see which ones might impact your brand or even provide an opportunity to tag along with it, e.g.:

- **Cultural trends**

    o People say they want to eat healthier, but obesity numbers continue to rise.
    o Working at home is a growing trend.
    o Luxury is being redefined more in terms of "what you've done" and less in terms of "what you've got."

- **Demographics**

    o Boomers will try anything to look younger and live longer.
    o Couples getting married later and after they have children.
    o Younger generations are more skeptical about traditional marketing claims.

- **Government policy**

    o Greater demand for energy self-sufficiency.
    o Pressure to reduce healthcare costs.
    o Tighter regulations for banks.

- **Technology**

  o Residential telephone landlines becoming a thing of the past.
  o Web 3.0 and mobile marketing will change everything.
  o The rapid rise of Cloud computing.

- **Industry trends**

  o Big corporations are taking corporate social responsibility more seriously.
  o What is the 900lb gorilla in the market planning for the future?
  o Continuing pressure on CPG brands from private labels.

These are just some of the "usual suspects"; there will be more depending on the category your brand competes in.

So on to specifics:

Step 1: Brainstorm the key cultural and macro trends that are likely to impact your brand in the next five to 10 years, and capture them as bullet point headlines.

Step 2: Sort them into two categories: opportunities and threats. Most of the points will fall into one or the other of these categories; if one of the points could be both, put it into both lists.

Step 3: Now prioritize the list of opportunities on the basis of greatest potential impact on your brand in the next five to 10 years using Power Dots (see Appendix 2).

Step 4: Ditto for the threats.

Now with the Future nailed down, you've completed the sixth of the eight exercises required to define your brand strategy.

Capturing the Future in this way identifies the cultural and macro trends your brand needs to anticipate and establishes another benchmark by which you can evaluate your eventual Future Brand Essence statement.

Summary:

- The future opportunities and threats exercise summarizes the key cultural and macro trends that could impact your brand in the future.

- At bare minimum, examine the "usual suspects" such as cultural trends, demographics, government policy, technology and industry trends.

- Brainstorm your headlines as bullet points – don't try to capture long speeches – then verify and prioritize them as two lists: opportunities and threats.

- Future opportunities and threats will serve as a key benchmark in evaluating candidate Future Brand Essence statements.

10

Future Brand Essence

Introducing the concept of Future Brand Essence and sharing examples. Reviewing the Brand Mirror™. Extracting and distilling the desired DNA of the brand. Key criteria to be met. Why stealing is good. Strategies for gaining consensus and closure.

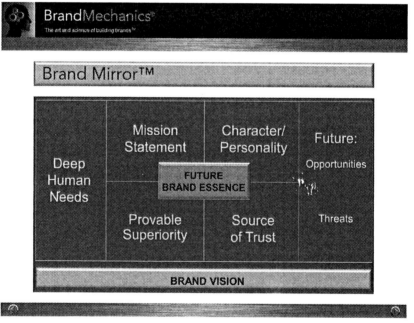

Now the heavy lifting begins.

You've completed the six preliminary exercises to construct the BrandMechanics® Brand Mirror™. In a one-day offsite brand workshop, this will typically take most of the morning, around four hours.

By building the Brand Mirror™ step by step and taking the time to generate, discuss, debate, amend and where appropriate prioritize the output, you now have consensus on the core elements of your Brand Strategy.

You've created a lot of useful, compressed, rich language that describes these key components, and now it's time to leverage this language as we reach for the center of gravity of the Mirror – the Future Brand Essence, a.k.a. the Desired Brand DNA, the heart and soul of what your brand will become.

For practical purposes when working with a group, I always capture the output from each of the six morning exercises on flip charts and then stage-by-stage build the Mirror on a blank wall so everyone can see the work and can refer to it during the rest of the day.

> Build the Mirror on a blank wall so everyone can see the work.

Before starting the heavy lifting, it's helpful to discuss the form that Future Brand Essence statements take.

To do that, I share about 20 FBE statements with the group so participants can get a better feel for what they are being asked to do in this exercise.

A couple of examples:

Marlboro: *Ruggedness. Masculinity. Independence.*

Let's put away our distaste for tobacco for a second and understand that these three simple words formed the bedrock of one of the most successful brands of the 20th century.

As expressed through the iconic cowboy, who clearly embodied the brand's essence, the brand itself was favored by men and women across all cultures and in all countries.

And its appeal was purely emotional with no rational underpinning whatsoever.

Notice also that the essence statement was never used as a tagline. A brand essence is what the brand stands for and therefore can be used as the inspiration for a tagline. But in most cases (with some exceptions) the brand essence is not a tagline but an internal mantra, a strategic summation of the brand's power.

Palo Alto University: *Engaging minds, improving lives.*

PAU is dedicated to the social sciences with a strong emphasis on clinical psychology and strong ties to Stanford University.

Four constituencies participated in the Brand Audit and Brand Workshop, each with their own unique perspective:

- ○ Faculty
- ○ Students
- ○ Trustees
- ○ Administration staff

Engaging minds reflects not only that PAU is a teaching institution, but also the fact that, unlike many universities, the faculty truly engages with the undergraduate students – not just the graduate students.

It also serves as a reminder that the four constituencies need to collaborate much more than they have done previously and need to sustain their outreach efforts to the community. So the "minds" refer not just to the students but the constituencies also.

Improving lives is a clear statement of what PAU does. It refers not only to the "cohort" system of teamwork they use to improve the education of their students, but also to PAU's commitment to improving the lives of the community they serve with their fully functioning outpatient clinic – one of the unique aspects of this institution. Improving lives also reflects their long-term commitment to the social sciences.

Finally, *Engaging minds, improving lives* proved to be one of the exceptions to the rule described above in that PAU adopted it as their tagline and have incorporated it into their logo.

Altus Learning Systems: *Knowledge on Demand.*

ALS was designed to break out of the old paradigm of "training" which might be summed up as imparting a lot of knowledge to trainees and helping them retain it.

> How to capture the intellectual capital of a company's experts and make it easily accessible?

Rather difficult to achieve however, when for example you're a company selling many thousands of different technical products and components.

The broader issue was: How to capture the IC (intellectual capital) of a company's experts?

ALS's approach was to video-capture company experts explaining individual products, and then to have those videos, with accompanying synchronized PowerPoint presentations, easily accessible online to those who needed the information – for example a sales representative preparing for a sales pitch.

The principal strengths of ALS were video production and the efficient searchability of the intellectual capital database.

Knowledge on Demand reflects those two strengths and makes a compelling promise to deliver the company's IC online any time of the day or night. It's also in synch with today's "on demand" business world.

These three examples, taken from B2C, B2B and education categories demonstrate there is no fixed form for writing a brand essence statement.

As we have seen, it can be two words or three words or a simple sentence. In fact, it can even be a single word or a couple of very short sentences.

The key thing is that your brand essence statement needs to be short and memorable, and it needs to sum up the heart, soul and spirit of your brand.

> **Recognizing** something is much easier than *defining* it.

Sounds simple, right?

It's certainly tempting to read the above examples and conclude that two or three words or a simple sentence must be pretty easy to write.

But you'd be wrong.

Because *recognizing* something is much easier than *defining* it.

Take your best friend as an example. Very easy for you to recognize. But now try and define that person in words. Much harder.

And brands are much the same in this respect: easy to recognize, harder to define. And that's why having a process such as the FBE™ methodology is useful – it will help and enable you to define your brand succinctly.

Of course you recognize your pet, but how would you define her in a focused, inspiring way?

So before we get into defining your brand's essence, let's try some simple warm-up exercises involving famous cities. In a group setting, you can ask participants to either work independently or work in small teams, then compare notes afterwards.

Exercise 1: Paris. Take a couple of minutes and write down what comes to mind when you think of Paris. Now can you sum up Paris in just a few words or a simple sentence?

Exercise 2: Los Angeles. Same exercise. What comes to mind when you think of Los Angeles? Write down the first things that come into your head. Again, can you sum up Los Angeles in just a few words or a simple sentence?

Exercise 3: New York City. Ditto.
Answers to these exercises are coming up shortly – so no peeking.

These exercises demonstrate that distilling a variety of thoughts and ideas down into a highly compressed set of words is achievable.

We now cannot postpone the "heaving lifting" any further; it's time to get down to the specifics.

Step 1: Review the Brand Essence statements referred to earlier in this chapter:

- **Marlboro: Ruggedness:** *Masculinity. Independence.*
- **Palo Alto University:** *Engaging Minds, Improving Lives.*
- **Altus Learning Systems:** *Knowledge on Demand.*

Focused, memorable, creating pictures in the mind and without a fixed format.

Also note that they do not mention the category in which they compete – mentioning the category is not necessary.

> Focus on what sticks in your mind and creates a picture.

And remember they are not tag-lines, which are creative interpretations of brand essence statements.

Step 2: Review the Brand Mirror™ you have constructed and feel free to amend anything that needs revising or just doesn't feel right.

Step 3: Silent exercise. Working initially as individuals, each participant now needs to write down at least one "first draft" of what they believe should be the Future Brand Essence of your brand.

I usually suggest 10 minutes for this and recommend that everybody reads and re-reads the Brand Mirror™ and tries to focus on what "sticks in their mind" and "creates a picture."

Undoubtedly Step 3 is the hardest part of the whole process because everyone needs to be working individually at this point – working in teams comes later.

Some participants will rise to the challenge and write multiple candidate statements.

It's not unusual however for some participants to get stressed and uncomfortable about attempting to describe the desired DNA of their brand in just a few words or a simple sentence. They might feel that other participants are going to scrutinize their ideas and disagree with them. Worse, they may think others might scoff at them. How we deal with this will be addressed in the next step.

Let me emphasize that participants feeling stress at this point is not only natural but also not a bad thing because it reflects the long-term importance of the task and the fact that this is indeed the hardest part of the process.

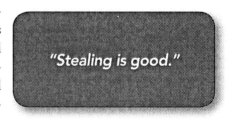

Step 4: Silent exercise. When participants are ready and have at least one candidate FBE statement to share with the group, they should write it/them on a flip chart so as to build a list of bullet points. The reason behind using bullet points is so that it is clear where each individual FBE candidate statement begins and ends.

As the list grows, I usually introduce the idea of "stealing is good." In other words, encourage participants to read the growing list of FBE candidates and, if they see something they like, then "steal" it and try to improve upon it. By "stealing" in this way, attractive ideas get played with, developed, polished and stretched into different areas. The general principle is that "stealing" is a kind of sharing and collaboration that will help with consensus building later on. So "stealing" is to be very much encouraged.

It's also important that this should remain a *silent* exercise, so no criticism is voiced.

Criticism at this important stage might lead to someone on the receiving end "shutting down" and feeling discouraged from contributing further, so it's best avoided – particularly if the group is highly opinionated and boisterous. Criticism in a constructive way will come later.

At the end of Step 4 you will have 2-3 flip charts filled with candidate FBE statements (two to three words or a simple sentence in each case).

Before moving on to Step 5, each flip chart needs to be labeled "Round 1" because there is typically more than one round before the final FBE statement is formally locked down.

Step 5: It's time to Power Dot. At this point as a general rule, I count the number of candidate statements and divide by three to calculate the number of Power Dots, subject to it being a maximum amount of five.

The other Power Dot stipulation at this stage is that no one can "vote" for their own candidate(s). This is important: Allowing everyone to vote for their own ideas could create a feeling of defensiveness. Voting for other people's ideas at this stage will generate a much better understanding of how the group feels as a whole.

It's also worth pointing out that this Power Dot session will most likely not be the end of this exercise.

Cities Exercise Answers:

There are no actual answers cast in stone, but having done these exercises over many years, these are the best ones that have emerged.

Paris: Most common answers: Romance. Fashion/couture. Art. Cuisine.

While the first three components definitely say Paris, there is sometimes debate over "cuisine" because it can be said to apply to the whole of France rather than just Paris.

Los Angeles: The best one I've seen is Smoggy glitz.

The physical reality of smog connected with the more abstract idea of superficial glitz (the Hollywood movie industry) creates a nice tension and a mental picture of a shiny veneer that's a little tarnished.

New York City: How about Ambition? Or maybe 24/7.

There's no doubt that NYC is about intensity which both these thoughts reflect. Other ideas that often arise are "Wired" and "9/11."

Another reminder: None of these answers is a tagline. Their intent is to represent the DNA, the heart, soul and spirit of each of these cities in a highly compressed form. Hence they might serve as a good basis for inspiring a tagline, but they are not taglines themselves.

Step 6: On a new flip chart, list in rank order the top five or six FBE candidate statements that appear to be getting some traction. Ignore for now the ones that did not attract many Power Dots.

Now review each statement against the following key criteria:

- Brief/memorable.

- Creates a picture in the mind.

- A "stretch" into the future – does it anticipate the future as expressed in the "Future" section of the Brand Mirror™? Does it exploit one of the opportunities identified earlier in the "future" exercise? Does it also broadly avoid the threats identified earlier? Does it represent something you want the brand to stand for in the future (rather than simply reflecting where the brand is today)?

- Fulfills a Deep Human Need – does it connect with at least one of the Deep Human Needs expressed in the Brand Mirror™?

- Is it consistent with the Character/Personality expressed in the Brand Mirror™?

- Not a tagline – avoid cute, folksy, silly.

As you review each statement, the goal is not to eliminate the various candidates, but to seek opportunities to improve them and generate even better ones.

> **Always capture new ideas: You cannot edit a blank page.**

During the discussion of each statement, participants will likely offer suggestions on how they could be improved or possibly combined to create better ones.

Be sure to ask them to write down their new ideas. To borrow advice from the screenwriting profession: *Always write down ideas before they disappear. You cannot edit a blank page.*

Step 7: You still have the five or six FBE candidate statements on a flip chart that have emerged from the group. And typically, each one has flaws but also has an idea worth pursuing.

It's also not unusual to see that several of the statements have some of the same ideas in common but have been expressed differently.

The task now is to capture what those core ideas are. I usually frame the question to the group as: "Some of these (five or six) statements seem to have some core ideas in common. Let's see if we can identify those core ideas."

With a new flip chart, capture the core ideas as brief, headline bullet points ensuring there are no duplicates.

Now ask the question: "Do we, as a group, agree that this list truly represents the core ideas we want to develop going forward and is there anything missing?"

Add to the list if necessary; delete the ones that are non-essential. Then discuss which of the ideas are the most important ones to retain for the brand. Power Dot the core ideas if necessary.

The author conducting an FBE™ Brand Workshop with the City of San Jose Green Initiatives Group.

Step 8: You now have:

- The five or six FBE candidate statements, in rank order, that emerged from the group in Round 1.

- A list of the core ideas, in order of priority, contained in the statements.

- New ideas that participants have been generating and writing down during the discussion of Round 1.

Time for Round 2.

At this point, the group can break into pairs of participants or smaller teams, but if someone wants to continue working individually, that's fine.

The task is broadly the same as Round 1: Each team needs to write at least one FBE candidate statement. Except this time they should build off the higher ranking candidates from Round 1 and develop them.

And again, "stealing is good" as this helps idea development and the consensus process.

Capture the new FBE candidates as bullet points on a new flip chart and discuss which ones appear to be based on the higher ranking core ideas.

Now Power Dot with the proviso that teams cannot "vote" for their own, and capture the top three or four that gain the most dots.

Step 9: If all is going well, you'll now have:

- The three or four FBE candidate statements, in rank order, that emerged from the group in Round 2.

- The list of the core ideas, in order of priority, emerging from Round 1.

By now the statements should be starting to "converge" and overlap in content and ideas.

It will also become clear that you can't force lots of ideas into a short, memorable Future Brand Essence statement.

So at this point, I might say, "There are still several ideas here fighting for attention. Which are the less important ones that we need to sacrifice in order to achieve a focused, memorable Brand Essence?" This is the *Issue Extraction* process

> **The key to achieving focus is *sacrifice*.**

(explained in more detail in Appendix 2) that will help narrow the field of candidates.

Sometimes there is concern and resistance to losing lower ranked core ideas. I usually address this with the Tennis Balls analogy I mentioned in Chapter 1 followed by a question:

The analogy: "Imagine I've got some tennis balls. If I were to throw you one tennis ball, the chances are you would catch it. But if I were to throw you three tennis balls at the same time, the chances are you won't catch any of them. Now the core ideas we're talking about here are just like those tennis balls. Too many, and they won't get caught. That's why we prioritized the core ideas."

The question: "So if you want to hold on to this (lower priority) idea, which higher ranked idea do you want to *lose* in order to make room?"

As I've said previously, the key to achieving focus is sacrifice.

Eventually, through a great deal of patience, you'll arrive at a "prime candidate" for your Future Brand Essence statement. But the process is not yet complete – you still need everyone to agree on it.

Step 10: Moving to closure.

The principal goal is within reach, but moving to closure on your Future Brand Essence can sometimes be a drawn-out affair as various participants dig their heels in and fight for their ideas.

And it's crucially important to have everyone on the same page so that subsequently all the participants are champions for the newly minted Brand Strategy.

Ignoring the concerns of just one participant and proceeding without them will set a time bomb ticking: One disgruntled group member can cause chaos later by openly expressing their disagreement and their disappointment of feeling disenfranchised.

So how to get the holdouts on board?

An effective way of achieving this is called *The Passion Meter.*

With your "prime candidate" statement on a fresh flip chart, explain the process:

Each person will be asked for a number between 0 and 10, where 0 means they think the prime candidate totally stinks and 10 means they think it is absolutely the best thing since sliced bread.

> It's crucially important to have everyone become champions of the new Brand Strategy.

As you go around the room, write the scores on the flip chart. So you might get something like this:

7, 9, 3, 8, 9, 7, 4, 8, 9, 7

Clearly, the holdouts are the 3 and 4.

So identify the 3 and 4, and ask them to explain their objections to the group.

Now identify the 9's and ask them to respond to the 3 and 4 and explain why they like the statement.

Then ask the 8's and the 7's to do what the 9's have just done.

When the ensuing discussion reaches a pause, then pose the next question to the 3 and 4:

"What would it take to get you from 3 and 4 to at least a 7?" It also does no harm at all to gently dial up the pressure with a glance at your watch and add, "We are getting behind schedule on this."

The dynamics behind this approach are that the 3 and 4 already know they are in a minority, so they might simply change their score and align with the majority.

Alternatively, if they are extremely passionate in their views, the majority may want to accommodate them with a tweak or two to the "prime candidate" statement.

If passions are running high in the ensuing discussion, wait for a pause and call for a 10-minute break to relieve the pressure and allow one-on-one lobbying to continue.

When finally you have something worth reconsidering, repeat the *Passion Meter* process and see how the scores change -- ideally upwards.

The overall goal of the Passion Meter is to have everyone's score be 7 and above. When that has been achieved, "lock" the Future Brand Essence statement by writing it in the space in the Brand Mirror™ you've created on the wall.

> The overall goal of the *Passion Meter* is to get everyone to 7 or above.

It's always a big moment; so I always suggest the group gives itself a round of applause.

Summary:

- Heavy lifting – potentially stressful initially, but it gets easier.

- Examples demonstrate shorter is better and there is no "fixed format."

- Participants should draft at least one candidate FBE statement each, then work in smaller teams.

- Silent exercises initially to avoid early criticism and "shutting down."

- "Stealing is good" – helps idea development and collaboration.

- Extract core ideas and prioritize them to establish benchmarks.

- Filter with key criteria.

- Tennis balls!

- *The Passion Meter* to help move to closure and satisfy holdouts.

- Close with the "lock."

11

Brand Vision

What kind of world or state of affairs do we want to bring about? What is your boon for mankind? Self-serving visions to avoid. Why Brand Visions are typically out of reach.

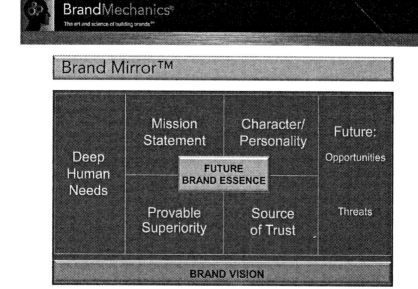

© 2013 BrandMechanics, Inc.

The "heavy lifting" is done: You have a Future Brand Essence statement expressed in two to three words or a simple sentence.

One last element remains to complete the Brand Mirror™: The Brand Vision.

The term "Vision" is used a lot in the world of brands and branding, sometimes loosely. The most important thing about a Brand Vision is that it should not be confused with a Corporate Goal.

So typical Brand Vision candidates to avoid:

- To be the most admired/respected company in our category.

- 10 million subscribers to our service.

- Revenues exceeding $100 million.

- IPO in three years, exit in five years.

- Overtake the market leader in two years.

Fine and entirely legitimate as Corporate Goals, but not Brand Vision statements, because they offer no benefit whatsoever to your target audiences and the world at large.

The best Brand Vision statements are those that evoke admiration and demonstrate the company wants to make the world a better place.

They should describe a future world or state of affairs that express a "boon for mankind," something that most people will agree is "a good thing to be striving for."

Some examples:

- **Standard Chartered Bank:** *A difficult and complex financial world made easy for you.*

- **Kraft Foods:** *Helping People Around the World Eat and Live Better.*

- **Office Depot:** *Delivering Winning Solutions That Inspire Worklife.*

- **Wal-Mart:** *Saving people money to help them live better.*

- **Microsoft:** *A PC on every desk in every home.*

Now look carefully at each of these and you'll notice they have something in common:

The future state of affairs described is clearly defined, but *has not been reached.*

For Standard Chartered Bank customers for example, the financial world is still difficult and complex, but the bank is committed to making it easy for them. That says something very positive about the bank and what's important to them.

The best Brand Visions are those that evoke admiration.

For Kraft Foods, clearly the world needs to eat better and live better. So good for them in pursuing that Vision.

What this tells us is that Brand Visions, by being future-based, are always *out of reach* and rightly so.

One of the roles of a Brand Vision is to get the brand stakeholders out of bed every morning to continue to reach for that better state of affairs. When that better world has been achieved, it's time to write a *new* Brand Vision to reach for.

So now to specifics:

Step 1: Review the Brand Vision statements referred to earlier in this chapter:

Each one is a simple sentence describing a future state of affairs you want to bring about – a world that contains a "boon for mankind."

Step 2: Review the Brand Mirror™ once again.

Step 3: Silent exercise. Working initially as individuals, each participant now needs to write down at least one "first draft" of what they believe should be the Brand Vision of your brand.

I usually suggest 10 minutes for this and recommend that everybody reads and re-reads the Brand Mirror™.

It can help enormously to frame the task as: Tee up the sentence with "We want to create a better world in which …" and then try to complete the sentence. Then when you have something you like, just remove the "teeing-up" part.

This part of the exercise, in terms of working individually, is similar to what was required for the previous exercise. But having nailed the Future Brand Essence, writing the Brand Vision is definitely easier to do.

Step 4: Silent exercise. When participants are ready and have at least one candidate Brand Vision to share with the group, they should write it/them on a flip chart so as to build a list of bullet points. The reason behind using bullet points is so that it is clear where each individual Brand Vision candidate begins and ends.

> Having nailed the Future Brand Essence, writing the Brand Vision is definitely easier.

Just as before, "stealing is good." Encourage participants to read the growing list of Brand Vision candidates and, if they see something they like, then "steal" it and try to improve upon it.

It's also important that this should remain a *silent* exercise, so no criticism is voiced.

At the end of Step 4 you will have one to two flip charts filled with candidate Brand Visions (a simple sentence in each case.)

Before moving on to Step 5, each flip chart needs to be labeled "Round 1" because there is typically more than one round before the final Brand Vision is formally nailed down.

Step 5: It's time to Power Dot. At this point as a general rule, I count the number of candidate statements and divide by three to calculate the number of Power Dots, subject to it being a maximum amount of five.

As usual at this stage, no one can "vote" for their own candidate(s).

And as in the previous exercise, this Power Dot session will most likely not be the end of this task.

Step 6: On a new flip chart, list in rank order the top three Brand Vision candidates that appear to be getting some traction. Ignore for now the ones that did not attract many Power Dots.

Now review each statement against the following criteria:

- A simple sentence.

- Creates a picture in the mind of a future, better world.

- A "stretch" into the future – something that does not exist today.

- Is it consistent with the Character/Personality expressed in the Brand Mirror™?

- Not a tagline – avoid cute, folksy, silly.

As you review each statement, the goal is not to eliminate the various candidates, but to seek opportunities to improve them and generate better ones entirely.

During the discussion of each statement, participants will likely offer suggestions on how they could be improved or possibly combined to create better ones. **Be sure to ask them to write down their new ideas.** To repeat the advice from the screenwriting profession: *Always write down ideas before they disappear. You cannot edit a blank page.*

Step 7: You still have the three Brand Vision candidates on a flip chart that have emerged from the group. And typically, each one has flaws, but they are reasonably close.

Usually with some tweaking you can nail down the Brand Vision statement to everyone's satisfaction. If not, then you'll need to go to Round 2 and have the group work in smaller teams to get to resolution.

> **The Brand Vision needs to be a stretch into the future – something that does not exist today.**

Step 8: Moving to closure.

Moving to closure on your Brand Vision is usually easier than doing the same for your Future Brand Essence statement.

But as before, it's important to have everyone on the same page so that subsequently all the participants are champions for the newly minted brand strategy.

If there are holdouts, use *The Passion Meter* as explained in the previous chapter.

The overall goal of *The Passion Meter* is to have everyone's score be 7 or above. When that has been achieved, "lock" the Brand Vision statement by writing it in the space in the Brand Mirror™ you've created on the wall.

Summary:

- Brand Visions are not Corporate Goals.
- Describe a future state of affairs that will make the world a better place.
- A Brand Vision is typically *out of reach*.
- When the world described is reached, then it's time to create a new Brand Vision.
- A Brand Vision is there to get stakeholders out of bed in the morning.

- Participants should draft at least one candidate Brand Vision each, then work in smaller teams.
- Silent exercises initially to avoid early criticism and "shutting down."
- "Stealing is good" – helps idea development and collaboration.
- Filter with key criteria.
- *The Passion Meter* to help move to closure and satisfy holdouts.
- Close with the "lock."

12

Now What?

We now have a Future Brand Essence and a Brand Vision. Now what do we do with it? Areas typically affected by Brand Essence. Why it's important to limit the number of ideas you commit to and to assign teams to champion the top initiatives. Keeping the outcomes under wraps.

Leveraging Brand Essence

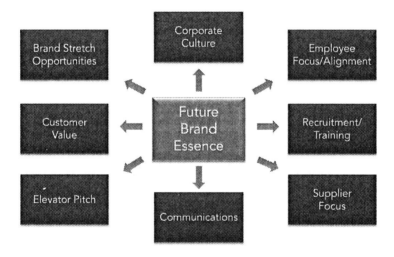

© 2013 BrandMechanics, Inc.

Clearly, your newly minted Brand Mirror™ and its centerpiece, the Future Brand Essence, have a broad range of leverage opportunities, all of which are important in their own right.

Corporate Culture

Your FBE needs to infuse your corporate culture and become part of everyday thinking and behavior. It should also impact your working environment.

If you are working in a dull gray environment with lots of cubes, brain-storm how the working environment can reflect your brand. If part of your FBE is innovation, a gray dull environment simply won't work.

Employee Focus/Alignment

If you have employees that couldn't take part in the Brand Audit and Brand Workshop, or perhaps your company or division has so many employees that it was impossible for all of them to participate, then sharing the Brand Mirror™ *and the thinking behind it* is important.

Don't fall into the trap of distributing a PowerPoint deck to all those not involved with the development process and expect that to do the trick – it won't work. See the next chapter for how to initiate the alignment of em-ployees and get them on board with the new Brand Strategy.

Recruitment/Training

One of the goals of future recruitment should be hiring people who fit the desired personality profile of your brand as defined in the Brand Mirror™.

So it makes sense for future recruitment efforts to incorporate the desired personality profile and to leverage the FBE and Brand Mirror™ in helping to describe the corporate culture.

And for training, every new recruit should be introduced to the Brand Strategy so they are clear as to what is expected of them.

Supplier Focus

Especially important for companies/divisions with multiple suppliers, ven-dors and strategic partners, sharing your new Brand Strategy with them will clarify where you are going and why, and will reduce any strategy misunderstandings moving forward.

Brand Stretch Opportunities

The Brand Mirror™ will act not only as an inspiration for diversifying your product/service offering, it will also act as a filter for new opportunities.

Customer Value

You'll have a brand valued by customers and create loyalty by being consistent to what you want to stand for. This applies in both B2C and B2B arenas.

Elevator Pitch

For your Elevator Pitch, the FBE becomes the anchor of your opening sentence to engage the attention and imagination of your target prospects.

The remainder of the pitch should then draw upon key elements of the Brand Mirror™ including the Mission statement (for what you will do for the prospect and the value you will bring), Provable Superiority to demonstrate why you are better than the competition and Deep Human Needs to demonstrate your understanding of the prospect's needs and motivations.

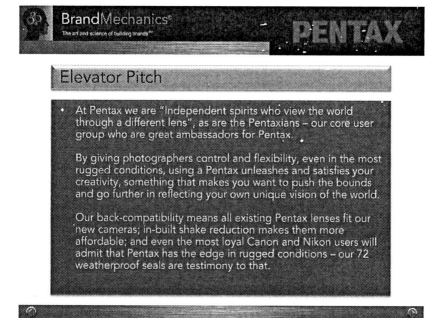

BrandMechanics®
The art and science of building brands℠

PENTAX

Elevator Pitch

- At Pentax we are "Independent spirits who view the world through a different lens", as are the Pentaxians – our core user group who are great ambassadors for Pentax.

  By giving photographers control and flexibility, even in the most rugged conditions, using a Pentax unleashes and satisfies your creativity, something that makes you want to push the bounds and go further in reflecting your own unique vision of the world.

  Our back-compatibility means all existing Pentax lenses fit our new cameras; in-built shake reduction makes them more affordable; and even the most loyal Canon and Nikon users will admit that Pentax has the edge in rugged conditions – our 72 weatherproof seals are testimony to that.

Communications

Communications, both traditional and digital, will be impacted by your FBE and the Brand Mirror™ in several ways, such as:

- A briefing document for all your creative resources/agencies.

- A benchmark for consistency of all external messaging.

- Tone of voice, as expressed in Personality/Character.

- Inspiration for messaging content, especially Provable Superiority and the Emotional part of the Mission.

- Thought leadership, leveraging Deep Human Needs and Future macro trends.

- Sign-off for press releases, especially the Source of Trust, to build credibility.

Clearly the opportunities just discussed, from corporate culture to communications cannot all be addressed in the context of a one-day Brand Workshop.

But what *can* be done, while everything is fresh in the minds of the group participants is to start brainstorming on what now needs to happen to turn the Future Brand Essence and Brand Vision into reality.

Another way of putting it is: What now needs to *change*?

Step 1: Building on the momentum you've achieved in the Brand Workshop, ask the group to divide into pairs and take a five-minute walk outside and come back with three distinct ideas for what now needs to change in light of the new Brand Strategy.

Step 2: Capture the ideas, one at a time, on a flip chart. There may be overlapping ideas, so de-duplicate as you go and tweak those ideas later with nuances if necessary.

Typical ideas that might emerge include:

- Share the new Brand Strategy with the rest of the company.

- Review all existing brand identity, collateral materials, digital assets, advertising, etc. and plan on making changes if they do not align with the new Brand Strategy.

- Incorporate the new strategy into the company's Strategic Business Plan.

- Change the incentives and bonuses program to reflect the new strategy.

- Re-imagine the office environment.

Step 3: Power Dot the candidate initiatives to prioritize them.

In order to be practical, I recommend you focus on just the top three initiatives (while making a note of the others for future reference).

Fact is, if you try and implement, say 10 different initiatives, it's quite likely none of them will get done. Trying to focus on a long list of initiatives can be immobilizing, so it's far better to focus on three that can be achieved in a reasonable time frame.

> Trying to focus on a long list of initiatives can be immobilizing, so it's better to focus on three.

Step 4: The three initiatives emerging as the top priorities now each need dedicated stewardship.

So invite individuals or teams of two or three to volunteer to take charge of each initiative.

Step 5: Each team's task is broadly the same:

Come back in a week with a plan, including timeline (and budget where necessary), and make the case for implementing the changes necessary to develop your brand.

The importance of these last two steps cannot be underestimated.

The excitement and momentum for change that have been generated by the completion of the Brand Mirror™ can easily evaporate if there is no formalized ongoing plan for internal alignment of employees and implementation of the first initiatives as a clear demonstration of commitment to the future of the brand.

One last thing to consider:

You've just defined your Future Brand Essence, and if you've constructed it properly there will be a lot of excitement in the group and quite likely a desire to share the workshop outcomes with everybody else in the company.

At this point you need to hit the "pause button" and ask yourself:

Do we want to just let everybody else know the results verbally while we're all pumped and excited?

Or:

Should we keep it all under wraps and share the outcomes, and the thinking behind them, in a more controlled fashion?

Once word gets out, the horse has bolted and will be hard to corral.

The grapevine a.k.a. the rumor mill will start buzzing. And if there are employees who felt they *should* have been involved with the brand development process but were not, they may start raising lots of unin-

Once word gets out, the horse has bolted and will be hard to corral.

formed questions which can then accumulate and start to spread cynicism and discontent.

Except with very small companies, my recommendation is usually to keep everything under wraps until the workshop outcomes can be shared in a controlled fashion and in an environment that demonstrates senior stakeholder commitment to the outcomes and all questions can be addressed.

And to do that properly, we need the BrandSharing™ process, which is the subject of the next chapter.

But before moving on, let's see where we are in terms of the overall Brand Building process:

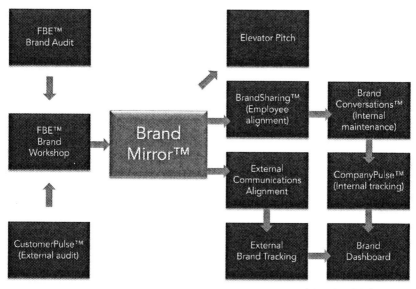

© 2013 BrandMechanics, Inc.

We've addressed the internal and external existing perceptions of the Brand with the Brand Audit and CustomerPulse™.

We've then taken all that information and used it as a springboard for the synectics-driven brainstorming in the Brand Workshop, leading to highly compressed language centered on the Future Brand Essence expressed in the

Brand Mirror™ which as a first step has been leveraged as an Elevator Pitch.

In the remainder of this book, we'll look in more detail at internal and external alignment, maintaining internal momentum, internal and external tracking and finally gathering together the key data.

Summary:

- Long-term impact of the FBE statement and Brand Mirror™: corporate culture, employee focus/alignment, recruitment/training, supplier focus, brand stretch opportunities, customer value, elevator pitch, communications.

- Short-term impact: *What now needs to change?*

- Brainstorm ideas/initiatives.

- Implement the top three to begin with.

- Assign individuals or small teams to execute the implementation of each initiative.

- Schedule a date to regroup and maintain the momentum for change.

- Keep all the Brand Workshop outcomes under wraps until you are prepared to share them with the rest of the company.

13

Brand Alignment

Aligning employees, internal processes and external creative expressions with the Brand Strategy. The BrandSharing™ process. Importance of Naming the Beast™ and the Slaughter of the Sacred Cows™. Challenging communications partners with The Passion Meter.

Internal alignment

First and foremost, it's important to resist the temptation to think that the alignment of employees and internal processes can be achieved by simply e-mailing the Brand Mirror™ to everyone in the organization and assuming they will read it, absorb it and act upon it.

It won't work.

Those employees who did not participate in the brand development process need to be able to fully understand it and feel ownership of it so that they can respond to it appropriately and enthusiastically.

So the goal is to get all employees on board with the new Brand Strategy, have them take ownership of it and have them align themselves as Brand Champions.

The BrandSharing™ Program

It may not be obvious, but one of the things employees will want to know is:

Why do things have to change?

Some employees may even be resistant to change, so having a consistent, well-thought-through reason for change is important.

Generally, change only happens due to an existing (or imminent) crisis or opportunity. So it's helpful to "name the beast" that is driving the change.

Typical things that can serve as a reason for change:

- Company expansion.

- Business acquisition.

- Intensifying competition.

- Market decline.

- Staff turnover.

- Customer dissatisfaction.

- Bad economy.

> It's helpful to "name the beast" that is driving the change.

Note that each of these is short and to the point, not a rambling sentence.

The Naming the Beast™ process is very simple:

Step 1: Gather the senior stakeholders of the brand.

Step 2: Come to an agreement on the reason for change.

Step 3: Ensure the reason is simple and to the point. The goal should be two words.

And if by chance you find you cannot agree on the reason for change, or you find there isn't a particularly compelling reason for change, make one up. I'm serious.

Every senior stakeholder can now be consistent when asked why things need to change.

Now it's time to start getting on board the employees that did not participate in the brand development process.

> If you find there isn't a compelling reason for change, *make one up.*

Preparation

The BrandSharing™ process requires a PowerPoint or Keynotes presentation using your company template.

You can construct it however you wish, but I've found the following structure works well:

- Introduction: Why things need to change.

- What is a brand?

- Development of the new brand.

- What we can do to support the new brand.

- Senior stakeholder Action Plan.

Introduction

A couple of slides on why things need to change.

If you've already completed the Naming the Beast™ process, this will be easy. A simple data chart substantiating the Name of the Beast will also be helpful.

What is a brand?

Feel free to borrow from the earlier chapters of this book. All I'll ask is that if you do quote from this book, please cite it on your slides.

Key points to cover:

- A brand is a set of memories/expectations.

- Branding is more than a logo or a label; it's also an internal organizational principle.

- Future Brand Essence is the desired DNA of a brand – its heart and soul.

- Strong brands have intrinsic monetary equity which can increase the value of a company way beyond its "book" value.

- Brand Essence examples.

Development of the new brand

The next few slides should be drawn from the Brand Audit report and include:

> Feel free to borrow from the earlier chapters of this book. All I'll ask is that if you do quote from this book please cite it on your slides.

- Both BrandAdvance™ results (characteristics and "doing words").

- Projective exercise results (today and future).

Next come the six Brand Mirror™ development slides, each one preceded with a set-up slide that defines the task and asks the question, for example, "What is our rational function and emotional role?"

- Mission Statement (rational function and emotional role)

- Provable Superiority

- Deep Human Needs

- Personality/Character

- Source of Trust

- The Future

Then two versions of the Brand Mirror™ slide:

- Brand Mirror™ *without* the Future Brand Essence included

- Brand Mirror™ *with* the Future Brand Essence included

What can we do to support the new brand?

This is a single slide saying just that.

Senior stakeholder Action Plan

This slide needs to briefly summarize the key initiatives agreed upon at the end of the Brand Workshop.

The BrandSharing™ PowerPoint presentation is now ready to go.

The next step is to schedule a one-hour meeting with up to 20 employees. If your company or group has more than 20 employees, schedule a series of back-to-back one hour meetings of 20 employees each.

The goal is to have every employee on board with the new Brand Strategy in the shortest possible time, so set aside a whole day or couple of days if necessary.

> The BrandSharing™ meeting invitation works best when it comes from the CEO and includes the word "mandatory."

Past experience shows that the invitation works best when it comes directly from the CEO and includes the word "mandatory."

It also helps enormously to have the CEO (or a couple of senior executives in their place) to give the meeting authority.

The BrandSharing™ Meeting

The ideal venue is a meeting room large enough to accommodate the 20 employees so that they can break into four groups of five people with syndicate tables to seat the teams with a flip chart and easel for each team to capture their ideas.

The meeting should kick off with a brief introduction from the CEO emphasizing:

- The importance of what the group is about to hear.

- Background to the Brand Strategy development.

- The time and effort senior management have already committed to the process.

- "While we have done a lot of the work already, we also need your help and input to make this work."

Time allocation: 5 minutes

The first two sections ("Introduction: Why things need to change" and "What is a Brand?") should be fairly self-explanatory. Feel free to quote passages from this book.

Time allocation: 10 minutes

Development of the new brand

First share the two BrandAdvance™ slides which demonstrate the need for change in both the way the existing brand is perceived internally (characteristics) and what it is perceived to be doing.

Before moving to the next slide (projectives), it's time for the group's first task.

Task 1: "If you had to describe our brand as it is TODAY as an ANIMAL, what would that ANIMAL be? Work in your assigned teams. You have two minutes. Be sure to write down on the flip charts what you think the animal is TODAY. Use your imagination and try to agree on just one animal if possible."

After the two minutes is up, ask each team in turn to present its thoughts to the room with a rationale behind its choice.

When each team of five has presented its choice, identify any consistencies between the animals and the supporting rationales.

Challenge the teams to use their imagination and try to agree on just one animal.

Then reveal the results of the projective exercise from the Brand Audit and again look for and discuss any consistencies between the results.

From past experience there will always be some consistencies and by highlighting them you'll be able to demonstrate significant overlap between the group's perceptions and those of the senior stakeholders.

Task 2: Repeat for the ANIMAL in THE FUTURE.

And by contrasting the "today" and "future" animals and rationales, you can re-make the case for the desire for change within the group.

Task 3: We now take the same approach for the Mission Statement (rational function and emotional role), except this time we ask two of the teams to work independently on rational function and the remaining two to work on the emotional role.

Again, when the results from the Brand Workshop are revealed, highlight the consistencies with the teams' efforts.

Tasks 4-8: The basic process is repeated for each of the remaining components of the Brand Mirror™. It usually helps to divide the tasks between the different teams to save time.

With all the components addressed, it's now time to reveal the Brand Mirror™ with the Future Brand Essence statement missing.

It's worth pointing out and emphasizing to the group that it took the Brand Workshop participants an entire morning of intense debate to reach consensus on all the components.

Note: If time becomes very tight, skip the last two components (Source of Trust and The Future) and simply share the full set of Brand Workshop outcomes with the group.

> By contrasting the "today" and "future" animals, you can re-make the case for change.

Task 9: "It's now time for the heavy lifting. Based on the results we have so far, we now need to come up with proposals as to what now fits into the center of the Brand Mirror™ – the Future Brand Essence.

"We saw earlier that there is no fixed form for a Brand Essence statement, but we know it needs to be short and to the point.

"Ideally, it should be two or three words or a simple statement that sums up the brand's desired DNA, and we saw some examples earlier that may be helpful to you.

"As you might imagine, this is not an easy task. At the Brand Workshop, it took us around two hours to reach consensus on the final result.

"So now give it your best shot, working in your individual teams and see if you can come up with the brand's future essence in the next five minutes – two or three words or a simple sentence."

At the end of the five minutes, ask each team to present their findings.

And again, highlight and discuss the consistencies between the results.

Now reveal the Future Brand Essence as agreed in the Brand Workshop and highlight how it manages to connect the various components of the Brand Mirror™.

Lastly, in this section, read the Elevator Pitch developed after the Brand Workshop as a demonstration of how the Future Brand Essence and the supporting language in the Brand Mirror™ can be leveraged.

What can we do to support the new brand?

Having gone through this highly compressed version of the Brand Workshop, the group should have begun to see significant overlap between their own thinking and the senior stakeholders' thinking and as a result feel some ownership of the new Brand Strategy.

Now it's time to turn that momentum into action.

Final task: "What now needs to change? What specific things can each of us do to support the new brand? Take a couple of minutes and working as teams capture some specific ideas and initiatives on the flip charts that will help us all get on the same page and deliver the promise of our new brand."

Ask each team to present their ideas and be sure to thank them – they will have done a lot of work in the past hour.

Get a sense of priority of the initiatives, focus on the top two or three and invite volunteers to form task groups than can plan and execute the ideas.

Lastly, reveal the senior stakeholder Action Plan and have the CEO (or their representatives) speak to how it is going to be implemented.

This is a good opportunity to introduce The Slaughter of the Sacred Cows™ which is essentially a dramatic gesture by the CEO to demonstrate that the changes being outlined are real and represent a break with the past.

> The Slaughter of the Sacred Cows™: dramatic gesture to signal a break with the past.

For example, let's say you are a bank, your newly minted Future Brand

Essence is "Making things simpler for customers" and currently your mortgage application form is 20 pages long.

Announce the formation of a new group tasked with creating a new application form that will be five pages maximum. Then with a flourish, tear up the old form.

It might sound corny, but it's what the meeting attendees will remember as a physical demonstration that things are changing in the organization and they need to be part of it.

In closing the BrandSharing™ meeting, ask the group not to share the Future Brand Essence statement with other employees until the full schedule of meetings has been completed. This will ensure the impact of the reveal of the Essence statement in subsequent meetings is not spoiled.

Just a quick example of how internal alignment can quickly generate new business:

A new social media platform start-up company had been struggling to get traction for about a year.

Their offering was highly innovative and parts of it were very technical and complex, and that was a big part of the problem: Their sales representatives were struggling to explain it to prospective clients in a simple, consistent way, and during the Brand Workshop there was a heated discussion on what was the best way to pitch the service.

Needless to say, the FBE™ Methodology delivered a focused Brand Essence statement which became the anchor of their sales pitch.

Less than 24 hours after the workshop, I got a call from one of the more vociferous and skeptical sales reps from the previous day, who told me they had just pitched a famous, iconic brand over the phone using the newly minted Brand Essence and in less than 30 minutes the client had asked for an agreement to sign.

So not only a demonstration of the intrinsic power of a focused Brand Essence statement, but also the transformational power of employee alignment.

And their business is booming.

> Gather all your communications partners together (including their senior creative talent) and plan concrete next steps.

External alignment

External alignment in this context means not only having all your external communications partners (including advertising/digital/PR agencies, design studios, etc.) on board, but also ensuring the external brand expressions they are responsible for actually align with the new spirit of the brand.

Ideally, your communications partners will have participated in the Brand Audit and the Brand Workshop, so getting them on board will be a done deal.

However, in the case where they have not been involved so far, the simplest solution is to schedule a two-hour BrandSharing™ meeting with them as a group and in the second hour brainstorm what steps each of them need to take to ensure alignment of your organization's external brand expressions.

And even if your communications partners were involved in the Brand Strategy development process, it is still a good idea to gather them all together and plan concrete next steps.

Given the importance of those next steps I'd also recommend they bring their senior creative talent with them.

Having reviewed the existing external creative expressions of the brand and then having reviewed the new Brand Strategy, the question is: What now needs to change?

- Brand Identity?

- ◦ Logo?
- ◦ Color palette?
- ◦ Fonts?
- ◦ Letterhead/stationery?

- • Messaging?
  - ◦ Tagline?
  - ◦ Advertising?
  - ◦ PR?
  - ◦ Collateral materials?
  - ◦ Web presence?
  - ◦ E-mail signatures?

Typically, working with the right communications partners, they will respond positively and align all the external brand expressions appropriately.

But on occasion there may be holdouts: Partners who feel perhaps their views were not taken sufficiently into consideration during the Brand Strategy development process and perhaps think they know best or even feel a little bit threatened by the new thinking.

Here's how one such instance played out:

The client was a high-end home builder and the Future Brand Essence we developed was based around their design creativity and the feeling of exhilaration expressed by their customers when seeing their homes for the first time.

Their ad agency had been fully briefed on the Essence and the Brand Mirror™ and I was sitting with the client senior management as the agency presented their latest campaign which was, frankly, the same old same old.

I was about to raise the issue of the new Brand Strategy when the president of the company spoke up.

Having recalled the effectiveness of the *Passion Meter* exercise in the workshop, he asked, "On a scale of 1-10, how well does this campaign reflect our new Brand Essence?"

The professional smile on the face of the ad agency owner quickly faded to become a look of panic as the room delivered its verdict with twos and threes.

Ouch.

A week later, however, all the smiles returned, and the advertising was on a new, exciting track.

> **The ad agency owner's smile quickly faded to a look of panic.**

And the president of that company continued to use the Passion Meter in assessing all the brand's new external expressions – something I continue to recommend to all brand stakeholder decision-makers.

Summary:

- Agree on the reason for change: Naming the Beast™.
- Prepare the BrandSharing™ presentation based on the Brand Audit and Brand Workshop results.
- Schedule meetings of 20 employees and engage them in the process.
- Slaughter of the Sacred Cows™ – the dramatic gesture that signals a break with the past.
- Brainstorm with your communications partners to identify what needs to change.
- Challenge them using the Passion Meter to keep them on track.

14

Alignment Reinforcement and Tracking

Use of Brand Conversations™ for internal reinforcement and CompanyPulse™ for internal tracking. Employee segmentation: Bystanders, Weak Links, Loose Cannons and Brand Champions. Involvement strategies to grow the Brand Champion segment. Creating a Brand Dashboard.

At this point you have created your Brand Strategy, including the Future Brand Essence, Mission and Vision; and through BrandSharing™ you've engaged all your employees with the details of the Brand Strategy in such a way that they should feel they are part of the brand's future and an essential part of its future success.

So you are off to a good start, but how to maintain momentum?

First let's consider the potential reactions from different employees.

Some may have clearly understood what the Brand Strategy is all about and want to do all they can to pursue the brand's goals, while others are more skeptical and would rather hang back and watch others lead the way.

Some may have got carried away in the excitement of it all and want to help but need guidance on the specifics, while for others the whole thing just went over their heads and they are at a loss to know what to do next.

In order to increase employees' understanding and involvement with the brand, a process of dialog needs to be initiated to maintain overall momentum behind the brand internally.

Brand Conversations™ is all about creating and sustaining the process of dialog.

> Brand Conversations™ is about creating and sustaining the process of dialog by reinventing the employee newsletter.

The idea of dialog within an organization may seem simple and obvious, but in so many companies that I've worked with in the past, the lack of internal communication has often been a source of ongoing complaint. I've regularly heard the following mournful refrain from middle managers: "Senior management never listens."

And often the complaint is justified.

The typical employee newsletter, regardless of whether it is hard copy or digital, is a classic example of "Management message distribution" – something that is *not* dialog.

Which is why Brand Conversations™ requires the reinvention of the employee newsletter as an important tool for maintaining internal momentum behind the brand.

The principle of Brand Conversations™ is simple enough:

Continue with the newsletter (digital is more flexible and efficient provided all your employees have Internet access) but *institutionalize the feedback* to create and sustain dialog.

And here's what I mean by "institutionalize":

All managers need to meet with employees reporting to them once a month. (I usually recommend that these meetings are scheduled as "pillars in time," e.g. "10:00AM on the second Tuesday of every month" or "3:00PM on the last Thursday of every month," so all participants understand clearly in advance exactly when the meetings will take place.)

The timing of the meeting should be synchronized to be two or three days after the distribution of the employee newsletter so everyone has had a reasonable opportunity to read it. In fact, the manager scheduling the meeting should make it a requirement that every-

> *Institutionalize* employee feedback to create and sustain dialog.

one has to read the newsletter before coming to each monthly meeting.

Each meeting can be structured as follows:

1. Discussion of the most recent newsletter (or multiple newsletters if distribution is more frequent than once a month).

2. Identification of the newsletter items that generated most discussion.

3. What feedback can we offer on those key items as they relate to pursuing the brand's goals? Any praise, criticism or ideas?

4. Anyone care to say:

    a. What the brand's goals are?

    b. What specifically the Future Brand Essence, Mission and Vision are?

    c. What the brand's Elevator Pitch is?

5. Let's look back at the BrandSharing™ meeting that everyone took part in and the ideas and action points that resulted. What progress has been made in implementing/maintaining those ideas and action points?

6. As you all know, the company's Employee Incentive Awards have been realigned to reward those employees who demonstrate the active pursuit of the brand's goals.

Anyone here with a great idea that could put them in line for such an award?

Now is your chance to speak up. There wasn't an award last month, so this month the cash total has accumulated to $500 … (This always gets employees' attention.)

When the meeting is over, the manager then completes a report form as a record of the meeting.

> **Cash incentives always get employees' attention.**

The report form could be hard copy, but ideally should be online and available on the company's intranet to simplify the aggregation of all the meeting reports.

The form itself should look something like this:

A. Names of manager and attendees.

B. Names of absentees.

C. Newsletter items that generated most discussion.

D. Feedback on those items including any praise, criticism or ideas.

E. Identification and understanding of the core components of our Brand Strategy by your group:
    a. Future Brand Essence: *Very Poor | Poor | Average | Good | Excellent*
    b. Mission: *Very Poor | Poor | Average | Good | Excellent*
    c. Vision: *Very Poor | Poor | Average | Good | Excellent*
    d. Elevator Pitch: *Very Poor | Poor | Average | Good | Excellent*

F. Progress/maintenance of the action points and ideas from the Brand-Sharing™ program: *Very Poor | Poor | Average | Good | Excellent*

G. Candidate ideas for the Employee of the Month Award.

By applying the Brand Conversations™ principles and having monthly meetings, scheduled as "pillars in time," you will ensure:

• Brand Strategy continues to be an regular topic of discussion.

- Feedback to the newsletter, which will itself when appropriate become the subject of further newsletter items which will encourage even more dialog.

- Employees are encouraged to remember and leverage the Brand Strategy, and are incentivized and rewarded for doing so.

- Tracking each month of the continuing generation and maintenance of ideas to support the brand.

Brand Conversations™, as its name suggests, keeps the conversation going about the brand.

And it's not unusual for major companies to require quantitative measures as a means of tracking their employees' evolving behaviors and attitudes towards the brand.

Which is where CompanyPulse™ comes in.

CompanyPulse™ is a regular online employee survey to track internal brand metrics including, perhaps most importantly, employees' understanding of and feeling of involvement in your Brand Strategy which will then lead to a unique employee segmentation.

> CompanyPulse™ is a regular online employee survey to track internal brand metrics.

Conducting the CompanyPulse™ program online with anonymous log-ins encourages candor and is the best chance of obtaining accurate data. And by incorporating a deadline into the web application, you will get prompt responses.

While it is not within the scope of this book to go into the detail of the survey questionnaire, it is nevertheless appropriate to share the kinds of output CompanyPulse™ can deliver.

Let's take the example of Guckenheimer Inc., a leading national corporate foodservice provider. Their Future Brand Essence is "Nourishing Inspiration" which reflects their commitment to creativity in serving healthy, nutritious, "from scratch" menu options, and in creating inspiring restaurant environments that encourage productive employee collaboration. (They liked their Essence so much that they decided to adopt it as their tagline.)

A couple of the questions they might ask in the CompanyPulse™ survey are:

- To what extent do you regard *yourself* as representing "Nourishing Inspiration" in the sense of positively encouraging co-workers to be creative in developing healthy menu options and creating/maintaining inspiring restaurant environments?

- Now, to what extent do you regard *the company* as delivering "Nourishing Inspiration" in the sense of positively encouraging employees to be creative in developing healthy menu options and creating/maintaining inspiring restaurant environments?

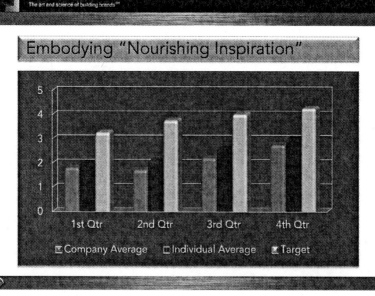

© 2013 BrandMechanics, Inc.

With both questions scored on a five-point scale, you can compare over time how employees score themselves and the company as a whole as living up to the Brand Essence.

Not only that, you can compare how different employee segments rate themselves.

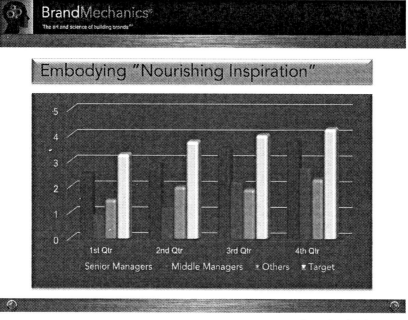

© 2013 BrandMechanics, Inc.

Another couple of the questions they might ask in the CompanyPulse™ survey:

- To what extent do you believe you fully understand our Brand Strategy and all that's needed from employees to make it a success?

- Now, to what extent do you feel you are involved on a day-to-day basis with our Brand Strategy?

With both questions scored on a 10-point scale, you can create an employee segmentation chart (see below) where the vertical axis represents "understanding" and the horizontal axis represents "involvement."

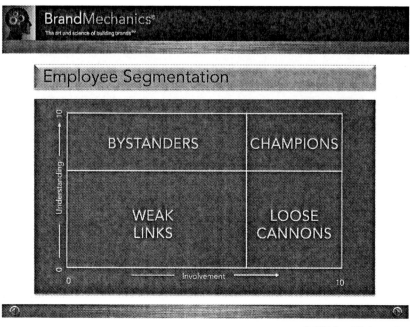

Obviously, the goal is to have everyone scoring 7 or above on both dimensions. When that happens, they fall into the category of "Champions."

Other categories include "Bystanders" – high understanding but low involvement. These are typically the cynics in the company who know what's required but don't want to get involved.

Another group is the "Loose Cannons" – high involvement but low understanding. These folks' hearts are in the right place, but they need help and guidance to better understand what is needed from them.

Finally, there are the "Weak Links" – low understanding and low involvement. These people are often newcomers who have not been through a brand orientation briefing yet.

When the data have been placed on the segmentation chart, it will look something like the one below.

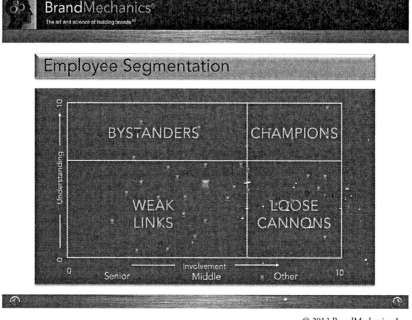

You can compare the results of the senior management, middle management and the others in the company.

(The larger squares represent the average scores of each group.)

And of course, you can clearly see how many Champions, Bystanders, Weak Links and Loose Cannons you have in the company.

Now as we indicated earlier, the goal is to have *everyone* migrate towards the "Champions" segment.

And while the Brand Conversations™ program will definitely help in this regard, it may be necessary to use specific involvement strategies for particular groups.

The first step is to invite all those who feel they are not yet Brand Champions to attend Brand Strategy briefings. These are very similar to the BrandSharing™ meetings but allow much more time for Q&A. Most of the attendees can be assumed to be Weak Links and Loose Cannons.

The most problematic group will always be the Bystanders, the cynics who are either generally resistant to change or who are disaffected with the company or who are simply unhappy in their work.

Given that the CompanyPulse™ program is conducted with anonymous log-ins in order to ensure candor, the Bystanders cannot be identified by name and isolated as a group.

And while it may be tempting to change the CompanyPulse™ protocol by having participants log in with their names, this will firstly likely compromise the candor of the responses, and secondly, the Bystanders themselves may see the "trap" being set and simply give false answers.

In reality, the attitudes and behaviors of Bystanders will eventually give them away, at which point someone needs to have a "deep and meaningful" conversation with them individually.

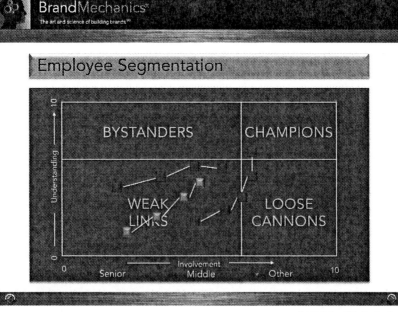

© 2013 BrandMechanics, Inc.

Now as the previous chart represents a single snapshot in time, you can compare the data over a period of time (see opposite) by regularly repeating CompanyPulse™. Hopefully, any diehard, residual Bystanders won't keep the individual groups' average scores from reaching the "Champions" segment.

Lastly in this chapter, I'd like to talk about Brand Dashboards, which are essentially at-a-glance comparative summaries of key brand and business metrics.

I typically recommend they are aggregated every quarter.

And they can be as simple or as complex as you wish.

The example on the next page shows eight key metrics:

- Latest Employee Segmentation showing the scatter of employees and the company-wide average.

- Quarter-by-quarter progression as the regional averages migrate towards the "Champions" segment.

- The percentage of Brand Conversations™ completed.

- Breakdown of Employee Segments.

- Social media mentions, showing improving sentiment.

- Quarterly improvements in Brand Preference.

- Similarly for Customer Satisfaction.

- And finally, overall sales.

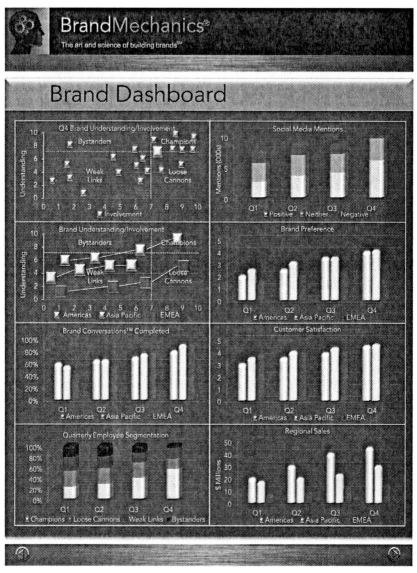

Summary:

- Brand Conversations™ program to regularly reinforce the Brand Strategy by creating and sustaining dialog around the brand.
  - ○ Managers and their reports meet every month at a "pillar in time."
  - ○ Newsletter (digital preferably) ceases to be a "Management message distribution" tool and is re-invented as a way of stimulating discussion and institutionalizing dialog.
  - ○ Monthly Employee Incentive Awards to encourage and reward brainstorming ideas that continue to support the brand.
  - ○ Managers file meeting reports including potential content for the next newsletter

- CompanyPulse™ to track internal brand metrics, including:
  - ○ How individuals rate their own commitment.
  - ○ How they rate the company's commitment.
  - ○ Employee segmentation: Champions, Loose Cannons, Weak Links, Bystanders.

- Brand Dashboard: At-a-glance comparison of key brand and business metrics

15

Quiz Time!

Some questions to help review the topics covered in this book.

Answers are in Appendix 5.

1. What is the difference between a brand and its messaging?

2. Complete this sentence: "Branding is more than a logo, it's also …."

3. What are the two important components of effective messaging in most cases?

4. Why are "strategy" and "positioning" potentially dangerous words?

5. You're asked who should attend the Brand Workshop. What do you say?

6. A CEO says she cannot attend the Brand Workshop because of a pressing engagement. What do you do?

7. You have the following equipment for the workshop: Computer projector, projection screen, electric extension cord with splitter, flip charts, easels, markers, pens, writing pads and toys. What are you missing?

8. What are the advantages and disadvantages of in-person internal Brand Audits?

9. Why are B2C and B2B External Audits often approached differently?

10. What are the essential components of a Mission Statement?

11. What are the two most important roles of Deep Human Needs in the Brand Workshop?

12. By what criterion do the Deep Human Needs need to be prioritized?

13. In the Provable Superiority exercise, everyone in the group believes they have a superior product. What do you say to them?

14. What is WCRS's famous mantra about product interrogation?

15. Why is the list of words/phrases used to define Brand Character/Personality limited to just five?

16. What kinds of words are best avoided in defining Brand Character/Personality?

17. What do you look for in the Source of Trust exercise?

18. Give an example of how the Source of Trust information can be used.

19. Name some categories where you might look for future macro trends.

20. In the Future Brand Essence exercise, why is stealing a good thing?

21. Name some criteria that the Future Brand Essence statement should comply with.

22. In the Future Brand Essence exercise, why is it important that members of the group initially work individually rather than in teams?

23. Why is a Brand Vision statement typically out of reach?

24. In the last session of the workshop, a list of 10 action points are generated and prioritized, and everyone is keen to implement them. What do you advise?

25. At the end of the workshop, what important decision needs to be made?

26. Name some of the areas which the Future Brand Essence will impact.

27. In the BrandSharing™ process, what is the difference between Naming the Beast™ and Slaughter of the Sacred Cows™?

28. What makes Brand Conversations™ different from traditional internal newsletters?

29. What are the four employee groups in the CompanyPulse™ segmentation?

30. What is the difference between an *Issue Extraction* and *The Passion Meter*?

Brand Mechanics

152

Appendix 1

Qualitative Research Tools for Brand Understanding

Brand Land

Ask consumers to close their eyes and imagine they have just been teleported to the land of the brand in question, and then ask them to describe the land in terms of what they can see, hear and smell. Also have them describe what is going on in the land.

Brand on Trial

Use this to understand the strengths and weaknesses of the brand by dividing the respondents into two teams – prosecution and defense – and explaining the brand is on trial. One team makes the case for why the brand should be discontinued while the other team defends it.

Obituary

Another good way of understanding a brand's strengths and weaknesses as well as its track record. Ask the respondents to write an obituary for the brand and pay particular attention to what will be missed.

Collages

Have the group participants choose magazine visuals that represent the brand and ask them to paste them together to create a simple collage. Repeat the process for the brand's key competitors, and then discuss why they chose specific pictures and what they say about the different brands.

POP intercept

Hang around at the Brand's Point Of Purchase (e.g., the popcorn fixture in the grocery store), and when a shopper is about to buy a particular brand, pretend you're not very knowledgeable about the category and ask them about the different brands, how they are different, etc. This is a great way to introduce interns and junior planners into consumer research.

Party time

Ask the participants to imagine that the brand and its key competitors are getting together for a party. Then have them talk about how each brand acts at the party, what their function is (host, guest, gate-crasher, caterer, entertainer, whatever), what they are doing, how they are behaving, how they interact with one another.

The Playground

Same as Party Time except now the brand and its competitors are in the playground. This is a great exercise for kids' brands. Ask the respondents to discuss what the brands are doing, how they are behaving, what toys are they playing with, are they on the swings, the slide or the climbing frame, who is playing together, who is playing alone, who is being a bully or a pest, etc.

Personification

Have the respondents describe the brand as a person in terms of:

- How they look
- The clothes they wear
- Who they hang out with
- Their gender

- The neighborhood they live in
- Marital status
- Their ethnicity
- Are they faithful to their partner?

- Their job
- Educational qualifications
- Introvert or extrovert
- Etc.

Deprivation

Brief the respondents not to use/consume the brand for a full week (the time period may vary according to the typical usage frequency) prior to the focus groups and keep a record in a diary noting how they felt and what they did on the occasions when they typically would use/consume the brand, what alternatives they considered, etc. Then discuss in detail at the groups.

Projection

This is essentially the same exercise described in Chapter 3. Ask the respondents to use their imagination and describe what the brand, and its key competitors, would be if they were an animal, a vehicle, a beverage, a retail store, a celebrity, a vacation destination, an article of clothing, etc.

Bring and Tell

Brief the respondents to bring to the focus group something that, for them, represents the brand (but not the brand itself). Then discuss why it was chosen, how it is similar to the brand and any other objects they considered bringing.

Story Time

Begin a story with "Once upon a time there was a brand named [brand name] that lived in the land of [product category]. One day ..." Then each respondent takes it in turn to add a new sentence in the story. After the last respondent is done, discuss why the brand did what it did, and any twists in the plot. Then repeat for the brand's key competitors.

\ppendix 2

nd Consensus Building

Synectics and consensus building techniques for use in Future Brand Essence workshops. Headlining. Building off and why it's important. Power Dots and controlling the Power Dots process. Issue Extractions: When and how to use them. When to use the Passion Meter. How to handle responses to Passion Meter results. Overview of consensus building.

Synectics

Synectics is defined in Wikipedia as "A problem solving methodology that stimulates thought processes of which the subject may be unaware." It was originally developed in the 1950s by George Prince and William Gordon.

Back in 1997 when I was the Regional Director of Strategic Planning with Leo Burnett Asia-Pacific, I met George Prince, and it was during that three-day intensive training session that my perspective on brand strategy development changed forever.

For although synectics in its purest form is essentially advanced, structured brainstorming and creative problem-solving, its application to Brand Workshops is as compelling as it is game-changing.

Up to this point, I had firmly believed that a consumer-driven, research-based approach was the *only* reasonable way of developing a brand strategy. After all, brands exist in consumers' minds, so how could anyone develop a brand

> Synectics is essentially advanced, structured brainstorming and creative problem-solving.

strategy without relying almost exclusively on consumers' needs, motivations, values, attitudes and behaviors?

So when I was first introduced to the concept of synectics and how it could be applied to brand strategy development, I was very skeptical indeed.

But after the synectics training session was over, I was a complete convert. I had a profound epiphany best expressed as follows:

- Consumers can help you identify where you're brand is *today*; they can't tell you where you want your brand to be *in the future*.

- Synectics is powerful way of efficiently leveraging the brainpower of senior stakeholders in the brand to identify where you want your brand to be in the *future*.

Two of the governing principles of synectics are:

- Separation of process from content, meaning the workshop moderator leads the process and everyone else generates content (although it's not unusual for the moderator to contribute content when appropriate).

- Separation of problem-solving from decision-making, which avoids the common problem in unstructured brainstorming where the two are mixed up together.

Other "rules" include:

- Headlining. Ideas need to be captured in compressed headlines rather than in dense detail. So when a participant spends five minutes expounding on an idea, my response is typically, "Sounds great. Now can you headline that for me?"

- No criticism. Nothing shuts down a workshop participant more quickly than immediate criticism of their ideas, so no overt criticism is allowed when ideas are being generated.

- Building off. It's always helpful to acknowledge that someone has helped you generate another idea by mentioning their name as follows: "Building off what Mary just said ..." The other use is when you disagree with someone's idea. Instead of criticizing it, say "Building off John's idea, and taking it in a different direction ..."

> The authorship of individual ideas is de-emphasized so they can be evaluated solely on their merit.

- Capture ideas. Even if it's a half-baked idea, write it down. Ideas can come quickly but can also disappear just as quickly. And you can't amend a blank page.

- Decision making. The process of decision making using Power Dots (¾" diameter dark blue sticky dots, available from most office supply stores) has several benefits:

  o It's a straight vote to determine which ideas the group wants to pursue.

  o The authorship of individual ideas is de-emphasized so they can be evaluated solely on their merit and not on who wrote them.

  o By doing the exercise in silence and encouraging the most senior members of the group to place their dots last, you minimize both the possibility of participants trying to influence each other at the last moment and the possibility of some participants being influenced by senior group members' choices.

  o Overall, the Power Dot process is an effective and time-efficient way of determining how the group feels as a whole about various ideas and helps build consensus around those ideas. It can also often have the added effect of privately signaling to someone they are in a minority, their particular idea does not have much support and is not going to go very far.

Three other important things about the Power Dot process:

- First, when the group has been generating ideas individually or in several small teams, it's a good idea to add the proviso that participants can't vote for their own ideas at this point.

  This forces people to fully consider everyone else's ideas and ensures that their own ideas will be fully considered by everyone else. It also avoids participants blindly defending their own ideas to the exclusion of everyone else's which can undermine the consensus building and can create potential conflicts.

  It's also worth pointing out in these circumstances that "Trading Dots" (e.g., "I'll vote for yours if you vote for mine") is not allowed.

- Second, understand that with each Power Dot session, you will specify the number of Dots each time, which gives you a certain amount of not only control but also discretion.

  For lists of headlines to be voted on, I usually calculate the number of Dots by dividing the total by three.

- Lastly, participants do not have to use all their allotted Dots – they can discard them if they wish; they are not allowed to put multiple Dots on one selection; and they cannot accumulate or save Dots between Power Dot sessions.

There are a couple of other techniques for helping groups make decisions and resolve conflicts, including *Issue Extraction* and *Passion Meter*.

> Power Dots are an effective and time-efficient way of determining how the group feels.

Issue Extraction is used when participants are trying to hold on to too many ideas and push them into a single statement such as a Future Brand Essence, Brand Vision or Mission statement.

The technique requires identifying, extracting and headlining in just a couple of words on a flip chart each of the individual core ideas in question.

Having extracted the core competing issues, review them to see if any contradict or are inconsistent with each other. If this is the case, invite comments of support from the proponents and opponents of the conflicting ideas and then come to a decision as to which ideas can be eliminated.

If there are still too many ideas, I usually remind the group that in order to achieve focus, you have to sacrifice and then repeat the "Tennis balls" analogy: If I throw you a single tennis ball, the chances are you'll catch it. But if I throw you several tennis balls at the same time, you probably won't catch any of them.

Eventually, you will reduce the number of core issues down to a manageable number of two or three. With the less important ideas eliminated, moving forward becomes easier.

The *Passion Meter* is used in different circumstances such as when you are down to a final statement but there are some hold-outs who feel they can't fully support it.

> The *Passion Meter* is used when you are down to a final statement but there are some hold-outs.

With your "prime candidate" statement on a fresh flip chart, explain the process:

Each person will be asked for a number between 0 and 10, where 0 means they think the prime candidate totally stinks and 10 means they think it is absolutely "spot on."

As you go round the room, write the scores on the flip chart. So you might get something like this:

7, 9, 3, 8, 9, 7, 4, 8, 9, 7

Clearly, the holdouts are the 3 and 4.

So ask them to explain their objections to the group.

Now ask the 9's to respond to the 3 and 4 and explain why they like the statement.

Then ask the 8's and then the 7's to do what the 9's have just done.

When the ensuing discussion reaches a pause, then pose the next question to the 3 and 4:

"What would it take to get you from 3 and 4 to at least a 7?" It also does no harm at all to gently dial up the pressure with a glance at your watch and add, "We are getting behind schedule on this."

The dynamics behind this approach are that the 3 and 4 already know they are in a minority, so they might simply change their score and align with the majority.

Alternatively, if they are extremely passionate in their views, the majority may want to accommodate them with a tweak or two to the statement.

If passions are running high in the ensuing discussion, wait for a pause and call for a 10-minute break to relieve the pressure and allow one-on-one lobbying to continue.

When finally you have something worth reconsidering, repeat the *Passion Meter* process and see how the scores change – ideally upwards.

The overall goal of the *Passion Meter* is to have everyone's score be 7 or above. When that has been achieved, "lock" the statement you're working on.

One last thing on the *Passion Meter*: I'm sometimes asked, usually after the event, whether I choose someone in particular to begin the voicing of numbers between zero and 10, or whether I choose the person at random.

And I must confess that on some occasions I've kicked off the process with someone who is likely to give a high number and who might positively influence the rest of the group. But does it really make any difference in the end? Hard to say.

Consensus building

I've referred to "consensus building" at various points in this book, and now is a good time to pull all those threads together with an overview.

First of all, having enthusiastic consensus among senior brand stakeholders is nothing short of gold dust, because it not only makes a clear statement of unity of purpose to the rest of the organization but also eliminates, or at least minimizes, future potential conflicts about the future direction of the brand.

I recall running a Brand Workshop for a start-up in San Diego several years ago. Two of the participants were the founder and the brand-new CEO.

> Having enthusiastic consensus among senior brand stakeholders is gold dust.

Both had egos bigger than a minor planet and during the course of the day there were several major disagreements between the two. Loud, ugly, stand-up rows that left the rest of the participants staring wide-eyed in silence.

Fortunately, I was able to corral the two by sticking to the workshop process and leveraging all the consensus-building techniques at my disposal.

We ended up with a clear consensus on their brand strategy, but to this day I wonder what would have happened to the management of that company if there had been no workshop and no consensus. My guess is the destructive rows would have continued, potentially paralyzing decision making.

Such is the value of consensus.

My goal however in the Brand Workshops is not just consensus but enthusiastic consensus.

And in order to achieve that, you must not only engage all the participants in the process but also resolve the various conflicts that will arise in a non-humiliating way so there are no losers in the negotiations, *only winners.*

The overall process of consensus building begins prior to the workshop with the Brand Audit.

The BrandAdvance™ exercises and the questionnaire analysis, conducted under conditions of strict anonymity, usually produce not only blunt, candid revelations of internal weaknesses to be confronted and addressed, but also compressed summaries of basic information (core audiences, strengths, etc.) that typically require not a lot of further debate. So the Brand Audit preempts potential conflicts regarding basic details.

Another way the Brand Audit helps is by including everyone with opinions about the future of the organization and the brand. By doing this, no one can complain later that their opinions were not heard.

The process of consensus building then continues with the workshop exercises in the morning as everyone has to agree on the results of an exercise before moving on to the next one. And every participant has the opportunity to speak up, so again no one can complain later that their opinions were not heard.

> All the workshop participants have the opportunity to speak, so no one can complain later that their opinions were not heard.

When the afternoon "heavy lifting" begins with the Future Brand Essence exercise, it's important that it starts with participants working individually rather than in groups.

This has the effect of not only demonstrating that it's a difficult task, but also that consensus within the group is going to be necessary to complete the task.

And when the Future Brand Essence exercise moves into working in teams, I regularly recommend to everyone that "Stealing is good." In other words, building off someone else's idea will develop that idea, move it forward and through the tactic of "stealing/sharing" it will help the consensus building as ideas start to converge.

The Power Dot process plays a big part in consensus building and resolving conflicts by ensuring each headlined idea gets a fair shake, minimizing consideration of who wrote which idea and helping participants who wrote subsequently unsupported ideas to move on without any feeling of criticism or humiliation. The process essentially levels the playing field and ensures everyone has a voice.

The *Issue Extraction* process helps build consensus by forcing choices to resolve conflicts and prioritize the key issues that need to be focused on.

> The *Issue Extraction* process helps build consensus by forcing choices to resolve conflicts.

And lastly, the *Passion Meter* exercise helps final resolution by ensuring no one's voice is ignored and by quantifying and helping raise the level of enthusiasm for the final statement.

So overall, consensus building consists of several components spread across the entire brand strategy development process from the initial Brand Audit to the final "lock."

And synectics, with its "rules" and goal of reducing of inhibitions to encourage everyone's creativity, plays a major role.

Appendix 3

Workshop Icebreakers/Energizers

An icebreaker at the beginning of the Brand Workshop (after the initial introductions and Brand Audit debrief, just before the first morning exercise) is particularly important with groups when some participants are meeting each other for the first time. A group that's having fun will work better together and generate more ideas and better ideas.

These mental energizers are also very helpful if or when the group gets stuck during an exercise or begins to get stressed or starts to run out of steam, especially in the afternoon.

The three essential components of a good icebreaker/energizer are:

- Concentration (to engage the minds of the group).
- Imagination (to get creative juices flowing).
- Fun (LOL and playing are great antidotes to tension and mental fatigue).

In an ideal world it's great to have one of these just prior to every workshop exercise, but they can easily cut into your timeline.

So I typically use one icebreaker to kick off the morning session and try to fit in two or three to restore/maintain momentum in the afternoon session.

Two truths, one lie

Ask for three volunteers. The task is for each individual to write down three things about themselves that are unusual and which the rest of the group will likely not be aware of.

It might be that you broke your leg as a child, or that you once met a famous person, or that you used to be in a rock band, or that you've been to the South Pole, etc.

> A group that's having fun will work better together and generate more ideas and better ideas.

The twist however is that each individual has to write down two things that are true and one that is a lie.

As each volunteer reads out their three things, the rest of the group has to vote as to which of the three things is a lie.

Ball throwing

Have the group stand in a circle with one person holding the ball. That person calls out "one" and passes it to the next person who calls out "two" and passes it to the next person who calls out "three" and so on until the circle has been completed.

Repeat but faster.

Now have the group mix themselves up and form a new circle.

Now No. 1 throws the ball to No. 2, wherever they are standing in the circle, who passes it to No. 3, wherever they happen to be standing, and so on.

Repeat but faster.

Object interpretation

Take an object and use your imagination as to what it might represent to you and then pass it around the room and ask each participant to do the same.

So for example a dinner plate might be interpreted as a satellite dish, a hat, a very large earring, a flying saucer, a large on-off button, a sporting trophy, a rather hard tortilla, the lid of a drum, a marksman's target, a large two-dimensional soap bubble, the moon, a manhole cover, a pizza, one half of an avant-garde brassiere, a warrior's shield …

Colored words

© 2013 BrandMechanics, Inc.

In this exercise, it's best either to have the chart projected onto a white screen or wall, or create your own in giant letters on a large flip chart.

Ask the group to recite together the words in order, just like they used to do it in 2nd grade (that's primary school for our UK readers).

Reading the words is pretty simple, so repeat but faster this time.

Repeat once more, faster still.

Now ask the group to do the same thing, only this time read the colors.

They will find it much harder and most likely start laughing because although it looks easy, it requires much more concentration.

Repeat a couple of times.

Storytelling in Three Words each

This is a fun exercise which, although simple in concept, continues to confound many group participants and leave them temporarily speechless.

Tell the group that you are going to start a story – it can be any story – with just three words and each participant in turn then needs to continue the story by adding just three words.

I always start the story with "Once upon a …"

It's always fun when people add twists in the plot and introduce weird and wacky characters out of the blue to make it more challenging as the story progresses.

If the story gets really interesting, you can always continue it for a second round.

> It's fun when people add twists and introduce weird characters to make it more challenging as the story progresses.

Competing storytelling genres

This is a more complex and challenging version of the Storytelling in Three Words.

Divide the group into three teams and give each team a storytelling genre to work with and compete against the other two teams.

For contrast I often use "erotic," "sci-fi" and "children's story" genres. So the exercise might evolve something like this, making each new contribution more of a challenge:

Team A ("Erotic'): *Very slowly, Mary began to remove her clothes …*

Team B ("Sci-fi"): *…as the inter-galactic cruiser blasted off from Earth.*

Team C ("Children's story"): *"Is it really time for bed?" said Johnny. "Now where's my teddy bear?"*

Team A: *"Johnny oh Johnny, I need you so," whispered Mary. Come to bed so we can get more comfortable. Pleeeeease!"*

Team B: *The spaceship shuddered suddenly as it reached warp speed and jumped into another galaxy.*

Team C: *"OK," said Johnny. "But only if you read me and Teddy a story. These spaceships can get really noisy …"*

Dog Cat Goldfish

You'll need a large open space for this exercise. Ask everyone to stand in the space.

Now ask, "What sound does a dog make?" and ask everyone to bark or woof like a dog as loud as possible for about ten seconds.

Next: "What sound does a cat make?" and ask everyone to meow like a cat as loud as possible for another 10 seconds.

> "What sound does a goldfish make?" A kind of "gloop gloop" noise.

And now ask, "What sound does a goldfish make?" This is usually a kind of "gloop gloop" noise, so have them make this sound as loud as possible for about 10 seconds.

Now for the interesting part.

Ask everyone to close their eyes tight and decide *in silence* which animal (dog, cat or goldfish) they would individually like to be.

The goal of the exercise now becomes: All the "dogs" need to *find each other* by barking or woofing loudly, and congregate in one place.

To do this they can't open their eyes and need to use their ears and their right hand to find the shoulder of another "dog" or group of "dogs" until all the "dogs" are together.

The "cats" and the "goldfish" need to do the same until all the "animals" have found their respective groups.

Slaps and Clicks: States of America

Have everyone sit with their hands on the table. (If there is not enough table space, participants can sit with their hands on their knees.)

To get started, call out a beat of "One, two, three, four; one, two, three, four .." having explained beforehand that:

On beat "one" everyone slaps their left hand on the table.

On beat "two" everyone slaps their right hand on the table.

On beat "three" everyone clicks/snaps the fingers of their left hand.

On beat "four" everyone clicks/snaps the fingers of their right hand.

Now that we have established the rhythm of the exercise, we explain the rules in more detail:

Now keep going until someone screws up ...

One at a time, each participant has

to maintain the rhythm with the rest of the group and name one of the states of the U.S.A. *over the clicks/snaps* of the fingers.

Now keep going until someone screws up and then start again with a different group of words. (Amazing how, with 50 of them, people run out of states to name.)

This exercise can also be done with other large groups of words such as animals, countries of the world, presidents of the U.S., chemical elements, etc.

Appendix 4

Puzzles

Brand workshops can be stressful at times which is why it's always a good idea to inject some fun whenever possible.

So typically I'll introduce a couple of puzzles at the very beginning of a workshop on the basis that if someone starts to feel stressed out, they can "tune out" for a couple of minutes and try to solve them.

Here are some of my favorites. Answers are in Appendix 6.

1. **Scotch on the Rocks**

   A man and a woman walk into a bar and both order scotch on the rocks.

   The man drinks his cocktail quickly and lives, while the woman drinks hers slowly and dies.

   Both drinks were identical. Why did the man live but the woman die?

2. **What word? (1)**

   What common nine-letter English word contains eight consonants but just one vowel?

3. **What is the next letter in this sequence?**

   O T T F F S S E ?

4. What letters should replace the ?? after the letter h?

a. RA   b. LE

c. AN   d. LE

e. YE   f. UL

g. OP   h. ??

5. Three Girls

Two girls are walking down a street when they see another girl. They turn to each other and one of them says, "That must be Kathy!"

They approach the third girl and it turns out they are correct, it is indeed Kathy, although they had never met her before.

How could they possibly recognize her and know her name?

6. What word? (2)

What English word has a string of six consonants in the middle of it?

Clue: It's a district in London.

Can you solve the following anagram?

"Chic bad manners."

7. Anagram

Can you solve the following anagram?

"Chic bad manners."

8. ML8 ML8

This puzzle is arguably the hardest of them all.

The number plate on a car is ML8 ML8.

In what country was it built?

Appendix 5

Answers to the Quiz in Chapter 15

1. A brand is a set of memories/expectations, a long-term benchmark for its activities. Messaging is what the brand owner wants to say today, so it's usually shorter-term in its scope.

2. " … an internal organization principle that can bring alignment to a company, division or group."

3. Emotional engagement and rational persuasion.

4. Because they can mean different things to different people in different circumstances.

5. Senior stakeholders in the brand, including senior management and strategic communications partners. As an extra filter: People who will make a difference both during and after the Brand Workshop.

6. If she cannot even commit to attending the afternoon session, postpone the workshop until her calendar is free.

7. Power Dots.

8. Advantages: Rigorous, comprehensive and flexible. Disadvantages: Not time-efficient (especially if interviews have to be rescheduled), potential lack of candor, not enough time for significant word sorts.

9. B2C Brand users are large sections of the general population, so the need is to recruit and audit a representative sample of those users. With B2B on the other hand, the user universe is often much smaller and directly accessible as a list of customers with phone numbers and e-mail addresses, so recruitment is much easier.

10. Rational function and emotional role.

11. Firstly, as a surrogate for target audience needs in the absence of an external Brand Audit. Secondly as a benchmark for your Future Brand Essence statement, which needs to fulfill at least one of the identified Deep Human Needs.

12. By the criterion of which Deep Human Needs the brand can best fulfill.

13. If you are unable to defend that claim in a court of law, it's out.

14. Interrogate the product until it confesses to its strengths.

15. Long lists of character/personality words/phrases are too easy and indiscriminate. Lists of fewer than five can be impossibly difficult.

16. Corporate words (e.g., global, successful), descriptors that need to be earned (e.g., trusted) and over-used words (e.g. passionate, visionary).

17. Firsts, superlatives, originals, positive media reports, bragging rights, etc. underpinned by numbers whenever possible.

18. Annual reports, sign-off paragraph in press releases.

19. Cultural trends, demographic changes, government policy, technology and industry trends.

20. Firstly, it flatters the person from whom you are stealing that their idea is good enough to develop further (which in turn will encourage them to generate more ideas), and secondly it helps the consensus-building process by having ideas with multiple "fingerprints" on them.

21. Short, memorable, inspiring, ideally differentiated, a stretch into the future, creates a picture in the mind, fulfills at least one Deep Human Need and anticipates the future.

22. So that each participant can truly appreciate how difficult it can be

to write a Future Brand Essence statement.

23. Because if it were easily within reach, there would be nothing to strive for and nothing would need to change.

24. Trying to focus on a long list of initiatives can be immobilizing, so it's better to focus on three. Then invite participants to take ownership of the top three initiatives.

25. Do you keep the workshop outcomes under wraps to share later in a controlled way, or tell everybody while you're pumped and excited?

26. Corporate culture, employee alignment, recruitment/training, supplier focus, communications, elevator pitch, customer value and brand stretch opportunities.

27. Naming the Beast™ is the process of agreeing what is driving the need for change. The Slaughter of the Sacred Cows™ is a dramatic gesture by a senior stakeholder in the BrandSharing™ meeting that signals a break with the past.

28. Traditional internal newsletters are typically a form of senior management message distribution, while Brand Conversations™ are about creating and sustaining internal dialog.

29. Bystanders, Weak Links, Loose Cannons and Brand Champions.

30. An Issue Extraction helps prioritize competing ideas and eliminate less compelling ones. The Passion Meter is for reaching closure on a statement.

Appendix 6

Puzzle answers

1. **Scotch on the Rocks.**

   The poison was in the ice cubes.

2. **What word? (1)**

   Strengths.

3. **Three Girls.**

   They are triplets who were separated at birth, hence they easily recognized Kathy.

4. **What is the next letter in this sequence?**

   N. The sequence is One, Two, Three, Four …

5. **What letters should replace the ?? after the letter h?**

   ER. If you group the two columns together, they each spell a word: arable, candle, eyeful and gopher.

6. **What word? (2)**

   Knightsbridge.

7. **Anagram.**

   Brand Mechanics.

What you can also do is create an anagram of the brand name that is the subject of the Brand Workshop and set that as a puzzle. They are easy to create if you go to: http://www.oneacross.com/anagrams.

8. **ML8 ML8.**

Germany.

"ML8 ML8" when spoken quickly refers to "I'm late, I'm late" which is a famous quotation from *Alice in Wonderland* said by the White Rabbit. So the car is a VW made in Germany.

Index

Alignment, 6, 113-114, 118, 121, 130-131

B2B, 16, 29, 34, 42-44, 92, 115

B2C, 16, 29, 34, 42-44, 92, 115

Brand Audit, 20, 22, 29, 32-35, 38, 40, 43-44, 56, 91, 114, 119, 149

Brand Conversations™, 135-136, 138-139, 145

Brand definitions, 2

Brand Essence, 1, 13, 15, 91-94, 101, 113, 124, 128, 130-131, 133, 141

Brand Mirror™, 29, 45, 59, 89, 94-95, 98, 103, 105, 107-108, 110, 113-116, 118-121, 132

Brand positioning, 14

Brand strategy, xi, xiii, 6, 15, 21, 31, 42, 52-53, 59, 65, 80, 84, 87, 90, 102, 110, 114, 116, 121, 132-133, 135, 138-139, 141, 143, 157, 163

Brand Vision, 46, 105-110, 116, 150

Brand Workshop, 19, 22-24, 26, 29, 31-32, 50-51, 53, 55, 89, 99, 114, 116, 119, 149, 157, 163, 167, 175

BrandAdvance™ exercises, 35-38

BrandSharing™, 121, 123, 125, 131, 135, 137-138, 143, 151

"Building off," 157, 159

Bystanders, 135, 142-145

Candor, 29, 34, 38, 139, 144, 164

Champions, 121, 135, 142

Character, xiv, 46, 69-72, 76-77, 109, 150

CompanyPulse™, 135, 139, 141, 144

Consensus building, 96, 157, 160, 163-165

Consumer research, 22, 29, 53, 55, 154

Elevator Pitch, iii, 17, 115, 120, 129, 137-138

Dashboard, 135, 145-146

Digital media, iii-v, 29

Deep Human Needs, 46, 53-56, 58-59, 98, 115, 150

"Doing words," 36, 38, 47, 50-51

Emotional engagement, 1, 12

External audit, 29, 40, 149

FBE™ Methodology, i, 19, 29, 45, 130

Focus, 20, 58, 101

Index

Ford, Henry, 54

Future, The, 46, 85-87

Future Brand Essence, xiii, 15-16, 46, 59, 85, 89-90, 95, 100-101, 103, 108, 113, 116, 118-119, 132, 135, 137-138, 140, 150-151, 157, 160, 164-165

Gossage, Howard, 11

Headlines, 40, 64, 83, 87, 99, 157-158, 160-161

Icebreakers, 167

Internal audit, 29, 33

Issue Extraction, 101, 151, 157, 160, 165

Jargon, xiv, xvi

King, Stephen, 2

Likeability, 69-70

Loose cannons, 135, 142-143

Los Angeles brand essence, 93-94

Messaging, 1, 7-12

Mission, 47-52, 115-116, 135, 137-138, 149

New York City brand essence, 94

Naming the Beast™, 121-122, 151

Paris brand essence, 93

Passion Meter, 102-103, 110, 121, 133, 151, 157, 160-162, 165

Personality, xiv, 46, 69-72, 76-77, 109, 150

Pillars in Time, 136, 138

Power Dots, 58, 65, 78, 84, 87, 96-100, 109, 117, 159-160, 165

Prince, George, 157

Product interrogation, 30, 61, 65, 150

Product parity, 63, 65

Propositions, 10

Puzzles, 172

Qualitative research, 54-55, 153

Quantitative research, 42, 54-55

Rational persuasion, 1, 12

Secret sauce, 64

Segmentation, Employee, 135, 139, 141-145

Shaw, George Bernard, 10

Slaughter of the Sacred Cows™, 121, 129, 151

Source of Trust, 46, 81, 83-84, 116, 150

Stealing is good, 89, 95-96, 100, 108, 150

Social media, iii, 29, 145

Superiority, 46, 61-65, 82, 84, 115-116

Superlatives, 81-83

Synectics, 119, 157, 165

Tennis balls, 11, 101, 161

Toys, 26

WCRS, 61, 65, 150

Weak links, 135, 142-144